Miniature Reef
AQUARIUM
In Your Home

DR. C. W. EMMENS

A beautiful minireef aquarium by John Burleson.

A magnificent, flourishing miniature reef aquarium. The main feature of this setup seems to be large, flower-like anemones. Photo by John Burleson.

Miniature Reef
AQUARIUM
In Your Home

DR. C. W. EMMENS

Distributed in the UNITED STATES by T.F.H. Publications, Inc., One T.F.H. Plaza, Neptune City, NJ 07753; in CANADA to the Pet Trade by H & L Pet Supplies Inc., 27 Kingston Crescent, Kitchener, Ontario N2B 2T6; Rolf C. Hagen Ltd., 3225 Sartelon Street, Montreal 382 Quebec; in CANADA to the Book Trade by Macmillan of Canada (A Division of Canada Publishing Corporation), 164 Commander Boulevard, Agincourt, Ontario M1S 3C7; in ENGLAND by T.F.H. Publications Limited, Cliveden House/Priors Way/Bray, Maidenhead, Berkshire SL6 2HP, England; in AUSTRALIA AND THE SOUTH PACIFIC by T.F.H. (Australia) Pty. Ltd., Box 149, Brookvale 2100 N.S.W., Australia; in NEW ZEALAND by Ross Haines & Son, Ltd., 18 Monmouth Street, Grey Lynn, Auckland 2, New Zealand; in SINGAPORE AND MALAYSIA by MPH Distributors (S) Pte., Ltd., 601 Sims Drive, #03/07/21, Singapore 1438; in the PHILIPPINES by Bio-Research, 5 Lippay Street, San Lorenzo Village, Makati Rizal; in SOUTH AFRICA by Multipet Pty. Ltd., 30 Turners Avenue, Durban 4001. Published by T.F.H. Publications, Inc. Manufactured in the United States of America by T.F.H. Publications, Inc.

CONTENTS

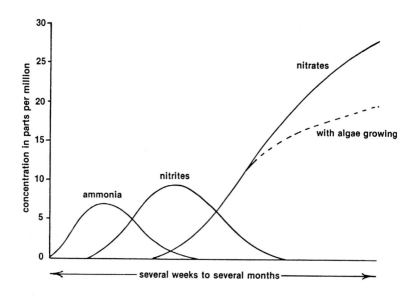

Changes in nitrogen-containing compounds which occur in a newly set-up tank. From THE MARINE AQUARIUM IN THEORY AND PRACTICE by Dr. C. W. Emmens.

Chapter 1
WHAT IS A MINIATURE REEF AQUARIUM?

Introduction

As our interest in marine aquarium keeping has expanded from the keeping of marine fishes to the more ambitious keeping of invertebrates and fish-invertebrate mixtures, the need for a closer copy of the natural environment has emerged. Fish-keeping in the marine tank taught us about the nitrogen cycle, discussed below. We found that in contrast to the average freshwater aquarium, the marine aquarium must be matured before many fishes can be introduced or the dreaded "new tank syndrome" would almost certainly strike. This happens because ammonia is produced and must be dealt with in one way or another. Although we now have substances available that can deal with the ammonia directly, they do not solve other problems. It is usual to depend on a biological filter in which the ammonia is converted via nitrites to relatively harmless nitrates. **Relatively harmless, that is, to fishes, but not to some invertebrates!**

Fishes are relatively tough. They can stand 20 – 40 parts per million (ppm) of nitrates and many species can tolerate much higher levels, even over 100 ppm. So can many crustaceans (crabs, shrimps, etc.), some anemones and tube worms, but other anemones, corals and many other types of invertebrate just fade away if much nitrate is present. There are other pollutants as well:

phenols, fatty acids, proteins, polypeptides and amino acids that will only slowly be converted to ammonia, if at all, and these affect the more sensitive invertebrates. In fact, although fishes can tolerate high concentrations of nitrate, etc., if you get them into purer water the improvement in color and sometimes behavior is impressive. There is a lot to be gained from better control of all possible pollutants in the marine tank.

Pollution is not the full story. The need for as high an oxygen level as possible is much greater in the marine tank than in a freshwater one, and again the improvement in both fishes and invertebrates when this is attended to is dramatic. Oxygen is less soluble in salt water than in fresh water, yet most inhabitants

The usual marine aquarium is like a desert compared to the living reef aquarium.

of the sea in which we are interested need high levels of it. It is also less soluble in warm water than in cold water, so that warm sea water holds much less than cool fresh water. At 50°F (10°C) each liter of fresh water can contain 8 ml of oxygen, whereas at 77°F (25°C) it can contain only 5.9 ml. At 50°F (10°C) sea water contains 6.5 ml of oxygen when saturated, but at 77°F (25°C) this drops to 4.8 ml. In the aquarium we rarely attain full saturation. Anything less than 3 or 4 ml/liter affects sensitive creatures and biological filters that are great consumers of oxygen.

The maintenance of high pH is more important to some invertebrates, such as corals, than it is to fishes and this must also receive attention. Carbon dioxide (CO_2) concentration and pH are inversely related - i.e. the higher the CO_2 concentration the lower the pH. Sea water is at pH 8.2 when in contact with fresh air, and varies normally between 8.0 and 8.3. In the aquarium it can easily fall below this range, even to 7.4 or so, that can be tolerated by most fishes but not by many invertebrates. Corals must stay above pH 8.0 to remain healthy.

Aquaria containing only fishes are often lit by a single fluorescent tube that proves to be satisfactory, whereas those housing algae, particularly macro-algae (higher forms with fronds and hold-fasts) need much more light. So do the algae that live in the tissues of invertebrates such as sponges, anemones, corals, clams and many others, upon which the animals are usually dependent. Both the quantity and the spectral quality of the light supplied are of primary importance.

So the simple answer to "What is a miniature reef tank?" is that it is one in which all these factors are controlled so that it may house

Under all circumstances there is an interplay between the fishes in the marine aquarium and all the other living things in the same aquarium. Reading books and magazines, experience, and talking to other aquarists and petshop managers are the only ways to achieve an understanding of the dynamics of the marine aquarium.

algae, invertebrates and fishes in a reasonably stable and healthy state with growth of most if not all of them. How to do it is what follows.

The Nitrogen Cycle

Proteins contain nitrogen and are a part of the food and tissues of all living creatures. They and their breakdown products are continually being released into the aquarium from uneaten food, decaying algae, the tissues and feces of fishes and the waste-products of invertebrates. These compounds are for the most part unwanted and act as poisons if allowed to accumulate. In an established tank, various bacteria break them down to simple substances, the most important of which is ammonium hydroxide, NH_4OH. Ammonium hydroxide dissociates according to the formula:

$$NH_4OH \longleftrightarrow NH_4^+ + OH^- \longleftrightarrow NH_3 + H_2O$$

THE NITROGEN CYCLE. The eventual accumulation of nitrates and other contaminants in the marine aquarium makes it highly desirable to control the nitrate content. Petshops sell kits by which you may measure the nitrate content of the water. Partial changes with freshly made marine water (10–20% every few weeks) is an acceptable remedy, but new filtration systems may make water changing unnecessary. From THE MARINE AQUARIUM IN THEORY AND PRACTICE by Dr. C. W. Emmens.

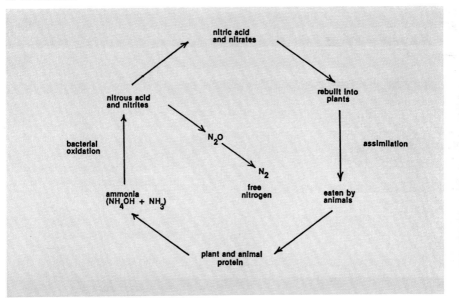

Dissolved gaseous ammonia, NH_3, is highly toxic to almost every animal, fish or invertebrate, and must not be allowed to rise above a fraction of a part per million in the aquarium. Unluckily, the higher the pH, the more the equation above shifts towards the right-hand side of the page and so the more toxic a given amount of ammonium hydroxide becomes. The balance is also pushed to the right as the temperature rises, but not so strongly. At pH7 (neutral) and 60°F (15°C) only 0.28% of the ammonium hydroxide is present as free ammonia, while at 80°F (27°C) the percent is 0.60%. At pH8 however and at 60°F (15°C) it rises to 2.75%, and at 80°F (27°C) it rises to 5.4% - nearly 10 times as much as at pH7. In sea water, at pH8.2, it is over 10 times as much. That is why the nitrogen cycle became apparent when serious marine aquarium keeping came about, whereas decades of freshwater aquarium keeping had not revealed it - although any sewage farm chemist or biologist could have told us!

The cycle involves the transformation by bacteria of ammoniacal compounds to nitrates, a process called *nitrification*. The first step is the oxidation of ammonium hydroxide by bacteria of the genus *Nitrosomonas* to nitrites (salts of nitrous acid, HNO_2), less toxic than ammonia but still toxic, and then further oxidation by bacteria of the genus *Nitrobacter* to nitrates (salts of nitric acid, HNO_3). Nitrates are readily absorbed by plants and so the proteinaceous compounds are rebuilt and start the cycle over again. Under certain conditions nitrates can be

Every marine aquarium is a living, active chemical reaction involving many variables. Aquarists are not able to cope with all the variables, but they should pay strict attention to accumulated dissolved gaseous ammonia and the process called nitrification.

broken down to free nitrogen gas, but this is mainly an anaerobic process that needs the absence of oxygen and different bacteria.

The Biological Filter

The bacteria just discussed need somewhere to accumulate. They will coat any available surface that isn't cleaned too often, but the interior of an base of the aquarium to filter the water through a thick layer of gravel (coral sand or the like in the marine tank) at least 3″ (7.5 cm) deep and return it by airlifts or power heads to the top of the

ordinary tank doesn't offer enough to help very much. Filter mats and such additives as activated carbon will offer an effective surface but are usually changed frequently and replaced with inactive new materials, as far as nitrification is concerned. It was discovered by R. P. Straughan that an undergravel filter works wonders in the marine aquarium, although he regarded it as a mechanical filter and actually resisted the true explanation of its effectiveness. The undergravel filter uses the

water. This of course offers a very large surface for the bacteria to settle onto and acts as an efficient biological filter as long as it is left undisturbed or at least only partially replaced at any one time.

Although an undergravel filter is very effective, particularly if seeded with the right kind of bacteria and fed ammonia from the start, it consumes oxygen and thus competes with the tank inhabitants unless the outflowing water is adequately reoxygenated. This is usually done by aeration of

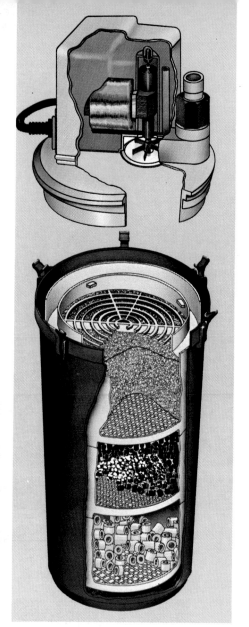

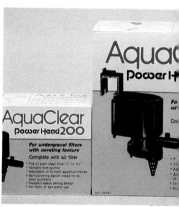

1 ↑

1. Power heads are attached to undergravel filters to increase the efficiency of these filters. The powerheads come in several sizes. 2. A closeup of a power head. 3. There are many motor driven filters. The Aquamaster has been on the market for a long, long time thus proving its acceptance. Petshops all over the world have many types of power filters and you should consult with the petshop manager to ascertain the size motor driven (power) filter best suited to your needs. 4. Undergravel filtration is extremely practical for many marine aquarium setups, including the minireef aquarium (under special circumstances). Petshops carry different designs and varied sizes.

Modern power filters, also referred to as cannister filters, can serve well in maintaining the minireef aquarium. As you can see from the cutaway view, this Fluval filter is capable of biological, chemical, and mechanical filtration. The various layers within the cannister can hold different filtering media.

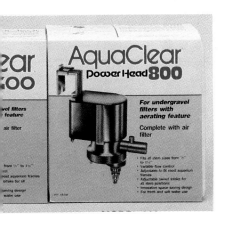

AquaClear Power Head 800

For undergravel filters with aerating feature

Complete with air filter

2↓

3 →

4 →

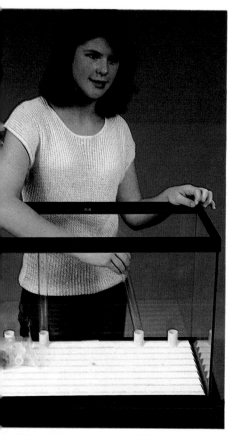

The use of an undergravel filter is limited, though very effective in many cases, particularly if seeded with the proper bacteria and fed ammonia from the beginning. The number and location of the outlets is important for the proper operation of the undergravel filter in each particular aquarium. It is better to have too many outlets (the excess can be shut off) than too few. Photo by Dr. Herbert R. Axelrod.

one kind or another, by returning the filtered water across the surface of the aquarium so as to cause ripples and good water movement, and by adding airstones. The filter can also be a nuisance since if any trouble (such as blockage) occurs, you have to reach down into the tank and disturb everything, a particularly undesirable process in a nicely set-up aquarium. So why not put it outside the tank, as in public aquaria?

That is what the minireef builders did!

Actually, European aquarists never liked the idea of an undergravel filter anyway. They tended to put all such filters outside. They didn't at first see the added advantages that could accrue. Not only can the filter be attended to much more easily, but it can be elaborated and made larger than an undergravel one. It can also be aerated so that the aerobic, oxygen-consuming bacteria work more efficiently and yet do not deplete the water of oxygen to the same extent. Further, you do not have to use coral sand or such, although many still do, because it has been thought to have the advantage of adding calcium to the water and correcting the pH. That is a mistaken belief since calcium does not dissolve from coral sand unless it is at less than a neutral pH.

External Biological Filtration

Simply placing the biological filter outside the aquarium adds to convenience, but not to its efficiency except that more layers can be added, or more compartments. To get more oxygen to the bacteria a trickle system is used, so that a mixture of air and water passes over them.

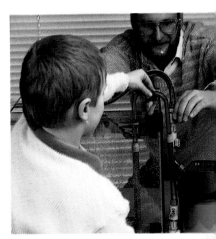

Petshops have a very complete range of power filters and the necessary accessories that go with them. If you are a parent, you should teach your child how to properly maintain a cannister-type filter as it must be cleaned regularly in order to keep it working properly. Clogged filters are worse than useless.

Oceanarium Products has marketed a simple but effective minireef aquarium with beautiful custom cabinetry and hidden filters. The filter, shown below, is basically the Dutch minireef principle greatly facilitated by American engineering. This unit is available at most petshops that specialize in marine fishes.

It is believed that by such a system the efficiency of the filter is increased nearly threefold. In the original Dutch mini-reef, a stack of four trays of coral gravel is used, each quite shallow. Water from the aquarium is sprayed over the top tray by a sprinkler tube and runs down through the gravel and a perforated base into the next tray, and so on. It then enters the first of four compartments situated below the trays, containing more coral gravel entirely submerged in tank water, passes from this into a second similar compartment, then enters a third compartment containing a layer of carbon as well as more coral gravel and finally flows into a pump compartment whence it is returned to the aquarium. The first part of the filter is called the "dry" part and the second submerged part the "wet" part, the whole constituting a dry-wet filter.

A more recent dry-wet filter system uses a double spiral of plastic matting placed upright and so constructed that it will not collapse and spoil the aeration. This is sprayed with tank water from a revolving sprinkler bar, the "dry" stage, from which the water then passes through 3" (7½ cm) of crushed coral, the "wet" stage, since the coral is immersed in tank water. This is then returned to the tank, or routed in part via a denitrifying system (see below). A somewhat similar system dispenses with the wet stage and

One of the main objectives of the wet-dry filtering system is the enlargement of the surface area within the biological filter which can sustain the helpful bacteria. This part of the filter is the dry part. In order to enhance the dry filter, Bioballs, Biobeads, or similar products are used to maximize the surface area of the filtering medium in any given filter. Beads run in sizes from a rice grain to a tennis ball . . . and larger.

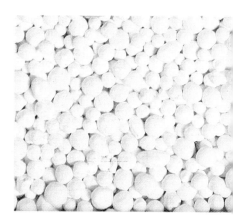

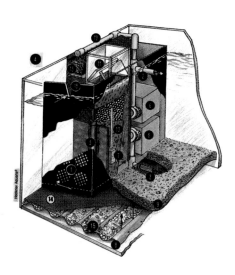

The Hockney Aquaria Filtration System
1. Filter Inlet. 2. Circulation Pump
Outlet. 3. Undergravel Filter Outlet. 4.
Aquarium. 5. Heater-Thermostatically
controlled. 6. Water Pumps. 7. Air
Diffuser in Contra-flow Compartment. 8.
Filter Plate. 9. Substrate. 10. Pre-filter
which slides out for easy cleaning. 11.
Protein Skimmer especially for marine
aquaria. 12. Bypass Spray Bar (Reverse
Flow Bypass System Only). 13. Dry
Bypass Filter, Wet Labyrinth Filter
Below. 14. Gravel Tidy. 15. Marine
Aquarium Buffering Agent.

runs the water over a stack of
Bioballs (or any other medium you
choose at your local petshop) in a
single large container. Bioballs are
light-weight polyethylene spheres
with a complex structure, offering
a large surface area (21.5 square
feet, or 2 square meters approx.)
per gallon (4 liters) of balls. A
volume of the Bioballs equal to 7-
10% of the water volume is said to
be sufficient for adequate filtration.
An airstone is fitted at the base of
the filter to ensure good aeration
in the final stages.

Denitrifying Filters

The processes that occur in an
aerobic filter can be reversed in

Petshops offer starter kits that feature
living bacteria for nitrifying purposes.

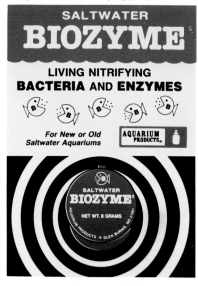

anaerobic (oxygen depleted) ones. Depending on the species of bacteria present, nitrate may be reduced to nitrite and to ammonia or to nitrous oxide and free nitrogen. The latter is what is wanted, and the free nitrogen gas will bubble from the water when its solubility is exceeded. There are many species of bacteria that are capable of denitrification and produce free nitrous oxide or nitrogen. Those from sea water have been identified as *Pseudomonas* and *Vibrio* species, but others can be introduced and function well. In contrast to nitrifying bacteria, most denitrifyers need a source of dissolved organic carbon to function. The most commonly used compound commercially is methanol, but this is toxic in the aquarium and is replaced by simple sugars, citrates or malates. Lactose (milk sugar) is often employed in marine systems.

A denitrifying filter must operate independently of the aerobic filter and, since it is depleted of oxygen, the water must be reoxygenated before going back to the tank. Further, movement through the filter must be slow since the chemical processes involved are slow. It is usual, therefore, to bypass a small proportion of the water going into the normal biological filter and to pass it at a gentle rate through the denitrifying one, then to route it via the biological filter and eventually back into the aquarium. The necessary lactose or other organic compound used is fed to the filter at regular intervals. The filter material may be anything suitable to act as a substrate for the bacteria, just as in the normal biological filter.

Incidentally, it has been found that areas of a biological filter suffering poor circulation may be denitrifying, an uncontrolled process that may happen to be beneficial by accident. However, the same areas may produce noxious substances like hydrogen sulphide and cannot be depended on to remain harmless. A recent product, the Nitrex box, utilizes this principle and contains granules of a substrate on which denitrifying bacteria operate and produce nitrogen gas. The box or boxes are buried in the substrate with an outflow left open or placed in unobtrusive regions of the aquarium and need infrequent replacement. All products mentioned are available at your petshop.

Special outside filters hang on the edge of the aquarium.

Algae

Marine algae, whether single or multicelled, need nitrogen to grow. They can manufacture proteins from ammonia or nitrates and sometimes from nitrites and other substances, depending on the species. Growing algae therefore act as denitrifyers and may be used inside or outside the aquarium to do this. Such a simple solution to the problem of reducing the nitrate level as growing plenty of algae in the aquarium has its limits because, depending on the numbers and weight of animals present, too much algae may be needed. In a rather sparsely populated tank, it is perfectly possible to keep nitrates below 10 or 15 ppm with a lush algal growth, but heavily populated miniature reefs, where the algae must be kept in proportion, are a different proposition.

In such circumstances algae may be grown in an algal filter, usually a shallow, well illuminated tray or trays over which water from the aquarium is passed and from which the algae are harvested regularly. The algae are grown on a bed of pebbles or such, or even on ridged plastic. Species such as the sea lettuce (Ulva) are very suitable. The alga Ulva lactuca has been shown to assimilate ammonia optimally at around 50 ppm while U. fasciata assimilated nitrates and produced maximum amino acids at around 800 ppm nitrogen, but of course did the job also at lower concentrations.

When both ammonia and nitrates are present together, seawater algae assimilate ammonia for preference, and thus tend to cut short the production of nitrate, a very useful attribute.

Quite a number of invertebrates, especially the corals and anemones and their relatives, house algae in their tissues. These may be blue-green, green, yellow-brown or brown algae - the zoochlorellae and the zooxanthellae. The typical alga of coral is the dinoflagellate *Gymnodinium microadriaticum,* a yellow-brown alga. The coral polyps produce enzymes that cause the alga to leak up to 80% of the products of photosynthesis and so feed the coral, while using the coral's own waste products plus others from the surrounding water to manufacture them. For photosynthesis, light is needed and the indwelling algae will only function and continue alive as long as they are adequately illuminated. If they are, they can feed corals or anemones, etc., so well that they may grow without receiving any other nourishment

This magnificent living minireef aquarium was made possible with the Lahaine System. All of the filters, heaters, pumps, etc., are hidden from view. This system, and systems similar to it, may be available through your local petshop specializing in marine fishes.

and help to purify the water instead of being a burden to it. The white anemones that you often see in petshops and home aquaria are usually ones that have lost their algae because of insufficient light, although there are some that are naturally white. These anemones do poorly even when well fed, probably because, in the absence of their natural symbiotic algae, they cannot rid themselves adequately of waste products. Such invertebrates when they receive sufficient light are therefore not a detriment but an asset to the aquarium in mopping up organic materials, especially nitrogenous ones, and in helping to keep the water low in nitrates.

Protein Skimmers

Some organic (carbon-containing) molecules adhere to interfaces. An interface is the boundary between liquid and gas or liquid and solid or solid and gas. In the aquarium it can be either of the first two, between sea water and gas or sea water and a solid. Protein skimmers or foam fractionators as they are often called utilize the former - sea water and gas, usually just air. A column of bubbles is sent up through a tube of sea water and the foam that accumulates on top is not allowed to escape into the aquarium but is trapped in a suitable vessel and discarded at intervals. The types of molecule that are collected are the surface-active or surfactant ones, and these include many of the dissolved organic compounds that are difficult to remove by other means - proteins themselves and their break-down products, coloring matter, phenols, and other substances that may eventually enter the ammonia-

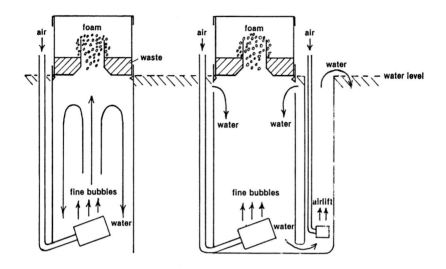

Two relatively simple air-stripping or protein-skimming devices. The unit to the right employs a counter-current principle, with water flowing against the air-stream. It is more suitable for simultaneous ozone treatment via the incoming air than the unit on the left. This drawing is based on a similar one in Dr. Emmens' book THE MARINE AQUARIUM IN THEORY AND PRACTICE.

nitrate part of the nitrogen cycle but haven't yet done so. Once they do, protein skimmers don't deal with them until a very high pH is reached - about pH10 or higher.

A protein skimmer can be of very simple design - just an airstone sitting at the base of a wide glass tube in the aquarium that has an opening above water level through which the foam rises and is collected in a cup. When the water is pure, little happens, but when it is really polluted a foul-looking froth accumulates and as the bubbles burst they deposit a deep brown liquid into the cup, that may need daily emptying. A more efficient design incorporates the counter-current principle by which the water is forced one way and the air the other, lengthening contact time and bringing untreated water to the top of the column where it meets bubbles already loaded with organics - a more efficient extraction procedure. Petshops have several models to show you.

The most efficient designs site the fractionater outside the aquarium and use a power source to turn over large quantities of both air and water in a long column much deeper than the tank. Studies have been made of optimal column diameters, bubble size, contact time, etc., with the result that bubbles of about 0.8 mm that do not come into contact with the walls of the reactor seem advisable, avoiding turbulence. However, much remains to be perfected.

Activated Carbon

Granular activated carbon may be used to adsorb dissolved organics using a liquid-solid boundary. The carbon must be in

the form of fine, dull granules of pin-head size that can be contained between layers of filter pad. Large, shiny pieces of carbon are not useful and may retain toxic materials that do harm. The granular form can be washed free of such matter easily, adsorbs up to a half or even more of its own weight of pollutants and may thus be used in quite small quantities. A few ounces per 100 gallons (400 liters) can be sufficient, to be changed every 3 months.

Samples of activated carbon differ considerably in their capacity to take up dissolved organics and it is difficult to assess these differences. This is not surprising since it may be made from wood, bone, coal and various materials and about the only thing to do is to depend on a reliable source of aquarium supplies that should have tested the materials it is selling. Alternately, a gas grade activated carbon purchased from a chemical supply company will usually be satisfactory but very expensive. Ideally, the container for the carbon should be a long cylinder, to give a prolonged exposure. Not too rapid a flow is desirable. However, just a layer

Ultraviolet sterilizers are based on the principle of exposing a moving stream of water through a field of ultraviolet light of intensity sufficient to kill all living things in the water. Ultraviolet-producing tubes have a rather short life (they just fade away gradually). Your petshop will advise you about the advantages of this type of sterilizer. Photo by Dr. Herbert R. Axelrod.

between the contents of an ordinary wet filter is more usual and as a result of continued recirculation of the water, a good enough extraction occurs. It seems to be a common misapprehension that used carbon can be reactivated by heating or by steam, but this is not the case unless 900°C is reached, as in its original preparation. As with protein skimmers, **carbon does not remove ammonia, nitrites or nitrates; they must be used in conjunction with biological filtration.**

Ozone

Ozone, or tri-atomic oxygen, O_3, is a mixed blessing and in fact seems to be used rarely in miniature reef aquaria. It kills off protozoa, bacteria and viruses and oxidizes a number of pollutants but it is a danger to tank inhabitants and even to ourselves if not properly handled. If used at all, it should be via a skimmer so that excess of the gas is not passed into the aquarium. For more or less complete safety, the water should be passed through activated carbon as well before returning to the tank. Direct release into the tank is not recommended.

Although there are circumstances when ozone can help to clean up a polluted tank it must be recalled that it is capable of oxidizing vitamins and other desirable compounds and so its

This lovely aquarium in Nancy, France received so much light that filamentous algae took over the tank. Photo by Dr. Denis Terver.

use is again problematic. If it is decided to try it, the dosage must be very carefully adjusted so as to do least damage and any detectable amount in the air of the room, which gives it an "electric" smell, indicates that too much is being used. Petshops sell ozonizers.

Ultraviolet Light

Sterilization by UV light is also rarely used in the home and must take place in a special piece of equipment in which a relatively thin layer of water is passed over the length of UV tubes so as to give good exposure. The UV rays are toxic to tank inhabitants and ourselves and so the equipment must be shielded. The range over which UV light kills bacteria is from 2000 to just under 3000 angstroms, peaking at 2600. The drawback with both ozone and UV treatment is that since the water should be circulated outside the

tank, material still inside the tank is not sterilized and so a complete job is never done. As it turns out, the environment of a miniature reef aquarium is so healthy that disease problems are rarely encountered as long as care is taken not to introduce diseased fishes. Even then, observation shows that many a fish, if left untreated, loses its infection spontaneously. Such measures as ozone and UV light are therefore rarely an advantage or necessity.

ABOVE: A very beautiful minireef aquarium. This type of aquarium is only possible with exactly the correct amount and quality of light. Photo by John Burleson.
LEFT: Ultraviolet sterilizers destroy almost all living things in water that passes through them. This keeps the tank more free of bacteria which cloud the water and disease organisms which prey on fishes. Photo by Dr. Herbert R. Axelrod.

Chapter 2
LIGHTING THE MINIATURE REEF TANK

There are such widely differing accounts of the light needed to maintain various invertebrates, particularly corals, that the subject deserves a short chapter to itself. Recommendations vary from intense illumination of 100,000 lux down to that provided by two tank length fluorescent lamps that would at best provide about 14,000 lux at the surface, probably somewhat less. Much depends on the nature of the invertebrates being kept. The reef-building corals top the list in light requirements with various other algae-containing creatures coming next. Others may actually shun the light, such as *Tubastrea* and other coral that inhabit sheltered regions and caves. Macro-algae also differ greatly in their light requirements but, in general, get on quite well in modest lighting.

Not only the quantity, but the quality of the light falling on the algae concerned is of prime importance. Whether we are considering algae directly or algae inside invertebrates, it is the light falling on them that matters. Algae respond by photosynthesis only to visible light. It is possible for ultraviolet light to damage or inhibit them. The primary photosynthesis pigments, chlorophylls a, b and c, absorb strongly in the blue and red regions of the spectrum and it might be assumed that a source of light yielding most of its energy in these regions would be best.

However, although a good output, especially in the blue, is desirable, there are other factors that complicate the matter.

The efficiency of a given amount of light varies in different parts of the spectrum and in

Petshops carry many kinds of lamps for the various aquariums. Marine aquariums, especially the minireef aquariums, require certain quantities and wave-lengths of light that are only available with special lighting tubes. Photo by Dr. Herbert R. Axelrod.

particular shows a drop towards the red. The presence of other pigments than chlorophylls can also seriously modify the effectiveness of a given wavelength. All algae contain chlorophylls, but many have pigments such as the fucoxanthin of brown algae and the r-phycoerithrin and r-phycocyanin of red algae. The pigment Beta-carotene is found in all algae. These pigments absorb light in various other parts of the spectrum, fucoxanthin in the central regions for example. They thus supplement chlorophylls and enable their possessors to populate deeper parts of the ocean where green algae, possessing only two chlorophylls and Beta-carotene, are at a disadvantage. It is factors like these that must be responsible for the finding that most marine algae grow well in cool white fluorescent light and that overall intensity and photoperiod are important. Photoperiod describes the number of hours each day of illumination and darkness, usually written for example as 14:10, light:dark. Most petshops sell various types of fluorescent tubes.

Light Needed by Algae

The average flux in daylight hours in the tropics is around 50,000 lux, reaching a peak of about 100,000 at noon - hence the very high recommendations of some authors. However, algae do not flourish at the surface of the tropical sea and the loss of light as we descend into the water is

The beautiful aquarium shown on page 26 looks like this from behind! Photo by John Burleson.

Aquarium Bologna, under the expert supervision of Mr. and Mrs. Werther Paccagnella, produced this magnificent marine aquarium in which all the gadgets are hidden from view in the pedestal.

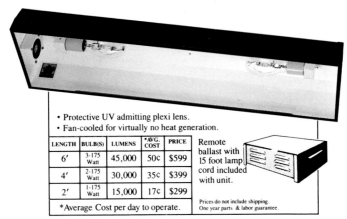

This Coralife Metal Halide Light, made by Energy Savers Unlimited, Inc. of Torrance, California, gave us permission to reproduce their ad (from TROPICAL FISH HOBBYIST MAGAZINE). It shows the possibility of imitating sunlight very closely.

considerable. At a depth of 10 meters (33 ft) only about 20% of blue-green light persists and less than 1 or 2% of red light, even in clear water. Yet this is the depth at which experiments with diatoms and phytoplankton have shown them to flourish best. These are yellow-brown or brown algae for the most part, related to the algae of corals. The flux at 10 meters must be around 10,000 lux or less, with very little at the red end of the spectrum. We shall see later that other experimental work with macro-algae lead us to similar conclusions to those reached with the unicellular types.

Measuring oxygen production by diatoms, Jenkins found that it increased with increased illumination up to 5,000 lux but not much further O_2 production occurred with higher intensities.

His diatoms were suspended in bottles at different depths in the sea, and 5,000 lux occurred at 15 meters (50 ft.). Above 5 meters (16 ft.) the production of oxygen fell sharply to less than half that at 10 meters. Measuring carbon fixation by radioactive tracers, Nielsen came to similar conclusions with phytoplankton, that showed a peak of fixation (i.e. photosynthesis) at 10 meters and a fall at lesser depths. The pigments in these brown algae are chlorophylls a and c, fucoxanthin and other carotenoids. There is a suspicion that the inhibition seen at higher levels in these experiments conducted in the ocean itself is due to UV light near the surface. Even if this turns out to be true, it does not alter the fact that the algae concerned do very well at 5,000 lux.

The top tank is a normal marine aquarium with no attempt being made to have it support anything more exotic than a few fishes. The bottom tank, however, contains living rocks which are starting to bloom. Which tank would you rather have?

Turning to the macro-algae we must rely on different types of experiment in which various investigators have reported on the light saturation values of various species. These values are the amounts of light above which no increased growth occurred. The general run of green macro-algae, including *Caulerpa, Halimeda, Penicillus, Udotea* and other genera needed 16,000 lux. Red macro-algae needed variable amounts between 1,600 and 22,000 lux, many of them (*Eucheuma, Pilayella, Plenosporium and Rhodochorton*) less than 4,000 lux. A single brown alga investigated, *Laminaria,* needed 3,400 lux. Remember that these are saturation values, and that the algae concerned would do quite well at half the figures or less.

So we come to the conclusion that various unicellular yellow-brown and brown algae and green and red macro-algae get along well with light intensities in the range 5-8,000 lux, probably less, and that none investigated can cope with more than 16,000 lux. In the ocean at least, more than this is actually inhibitory to algal activity and growth. However, what about the algae in corals and other invertebrates? Here we are at a loss and can only assume that they behave similarly. What nobody seems to have reported on is the loss of light when it penetrates the cells of the coral or other invertebrates. If this is significant, as may well be the case, the intensity needed may be greater than the available figures suggest. Most of the corals kept by aquarists are for obvious reasons those that open in daylight. These may well need less light than the majority of reef-builders that open at night and whose zooxanthellae are by no means exposed to advantage in the sun-lit hours.

Sources of Light

Most aquaria are lit by fluorescent tubes, but there is an increasing interest in metallic vapor and metal halide lamps, mainly by those who believe that intense illumination is desirable. Where fluorescents can or are believed to do the job adequately they are preferred because they are cooler and cheaper than the others. Other types of lamp must be raised well above the surface of the water or they cause

overheating. With a properly designed lamp this is not necessarily a difficulty as a spot-light effect can deliver high intensities to much if not all of the aquarium. Such a placement does mean that the space between the lamps and the tank top must be kept clear.

The commonly used fluorescents offer a great variety

of choice and one that differs from country to country. It is only possible to give general advice. Discuss with your petshop supplier the characteristics of any tube you may wish to purchase. Fluorescents may give anything between 1150 and 8500 lux at the surface of the aquarium. This is about half their total output as even with reflectors much light is

A minireef tank with special actinic lighting. Actinic-03 fluorescents are highly recommended as they produce the necessary blue end of the spectrum needed by chlorophyll-bearing organisms. Photo by John Burleson.

lost. Those, like Gro-Lux, that are designed to provide peaks of output in the red and blue and are deficient in the central regions of the spectrum, fall towards the lower part of the range. This is despite their being intended to stimulate plant growth and results in lower overall efficiency since it has been found experimentally that algae, unicellular or otherwise, grow well with cool or warm white tubes that give a greater overall output. Tubes with high output in the red and blue give a purplish light and make fishes and many other creatures look more attractive and have thus become popular, but this is not a recommendation for their exclusive use in miniature reef aquaria.

The lux output at the surface of an aquarium is one thing, but what about the depths? Sunlight is in parallel rays and falls in intensity as it penetrates the water because of absorption by turbidity or pigments in the water. A spot-light imitates sunlight to a fair extent, but a fluorescent tube does not and the intensity falls according to the inverse square law except for reflection from the glass. So 10,000 lux at the surface may be only 2,000 lux in the middle of the

Metal halide lights and halogen lamps give off considerable amounts of heat. It is best to have the lights far above the water's surface to prevent the water from overheating.

tank and even less lower down. Nevertheless, it is observable that plants like *Caulerpa* and *Halimeda* do quite well towards the bottom of a tank illuminated by only 1 or 2 white fluorescents. It is the corals and anemones, etc., that need the better lighting and these are normally placed so that they get it.

In comparison with the above, the output of 100 watt incandescent lamps can be as high as 9,000 lux; a 400 watt mercury vapor lamp gives about 90,000 lux but not all reaches the surface, particularly as its heat output is such that it must be suspended well above the aquarium. A 175 watt metal halide lamp gives around the same lux, but the same remark applies. These figures suppose that the light falls over a square foot of water surface (900 cm²). It would not apply to a single lamp over a greater surface but could be halved or more if such were used on, say, a 3 ft. (90 cm) aquarium.

The general concensus of opinion is that mercury vapor lamps are not suitable for marine aquaria because they produce the wrong overall spectrum. For

keeping reef-building corals, metal halide or actinic-03 fluorescents are recommended. The latter give an intense blue light needed by chlorophylls and so do not appear bright yet stimulate zooxanthellae. They are normally used in combination with other fluorescents. Metal halides produce a lot of UV light and should have a glass filter fitted to cut much of it out.

Common photoperiods are 12:12 or 14:10, in view of the near equal daytime and nighttime periods in the tropics. Some enthusiasts rig up equipment to give maximum illumination at mid-day by switching various lights on and off so as to imitate normal events. The importance of doing this has not been demonstrated, although it has been shown that constant illumination does not much increase algal activity compared with a 12:12 or 14:10 regime. Periodicity is important, whether or not more elaborate copying of nature matters. As with any aquarium, it is best to stick to a chosen regime and not to plunge the inhabitants suddenly

You can fake it! Plastic plants almost look like the real thing! This is a typical marine aquarium before the concept of the minireef became popular.

into light or darkness; this is best achieved by switching the room lights on before the tank lights and off after the tank lights, or allowing natural daylight to do the same thing for you. As most people like to enjoy their aquarium in the evening, during most parts of the year morning will dawn before you switch the tank lights on but you will have to take care of the switching off procedure.

Maintenance of Corals

There is clearly a lot to learn about the keeping of corals in home aquaria, but we can draw some tentative conclusions from the data available. Some corals, even reef-building ones can be kept and even grow in fluorescent lighting, or fluorescent lighting boosted with some incandescent lamps. Even more can be kept successfully with more intense lighting such as metal halides, but how many species will still fail remains to be seen. Some corals, even those known not to need much light and found in dim lighting on the reef don't do well in the aquarium whether lit well or not. Light intensity is certainly not the only factor, nor is genus or family, as some individual species are found to do well in families that in general do not.

The amount of fluorescent lighting used in the original Dutch minireef is about minimal - a white or daylight and a Gro-Lux type tube over a 60 or 70 gallon (230 to

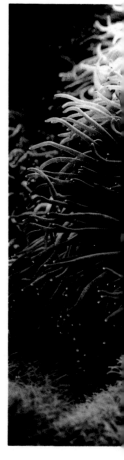

270 liters) aquarium, yet some corals survive. An interesting and prize-winning article by Donald E. Baker, Jr. (**TFH**, March '83, Vol. 31, No.7) listed his successes and failures with corals in an 80 gallon (300 liter) *natural system* aquarium - no filtration, just aeration and a 12% water change per month under 2 Penn-Plax Sea Lux 36″ fluorescents and 2

incandescent "plant growth" 25 watt bulbs. Of 23 species of coral tried, 9 failed and 14 survived satisfactorily and of these 5 actually grew (*Tubipora musica;* organ pipe coral, and four species of brain coral - *Favia favus, Favites abdita, Platygyra pini* and *Lobophyllia corymbosa*). Only a few of his successes open in the daytime and so that was not a

With actinic lighting startling effects are possible as the fishes and invertebrates thrive under almost sunlit conditions. Depending upon how much you are willing to invest, you can come closer and closer to imitating the real coral reef. Photo by John Burleson.

determining factor. For the Dutch minireef George Smit lists 15 stony corals that can be kept but implies that this is not all (FAMA May 1986, Vol. 9, No. 5). There must of course be many species that any one author cannot cite from hearsay or his own

experience. Baker's listing of successes as 61% of species tried is important as at least a rough guide to what to expect, even in a natural system, that is not claimed to be a minireef.

Despite their need of light to maintain the zooxanthellae, the majority of corals open at night and feed on the plankton that is then more abundant. One suspects that the strong dependence of such corals on light for health is tied up with the elimination of their waste products as much as it is with benefitting from the excretions of the algae. It is also tied up with calcium metabolism, as such corals lay down most of the calcium in their skeleton in daylight hours.

With the proper lighting and starting out with healthy organisms, it is possible to grow more than 50% of all corals, both hard and soft. Strong lighting is necessary even though many of the corals are only open for business at night. It really isn't necessary for you to experiment with corals and other living invertebrates. Your local petshop should be able to verify that a particular organism can or cannot successfully be maintained in a minireef aquarium. This Leather Coral was photographed by John Burleson.

Chapter 3
PUTTING IT TOGETHER

The various elements that may go into a miniature reef aquarium were discussed in Chapters 1 and 2, but not how they are fitted together in the complete set-up, or rather varieties of set-up.

There are three main mechanical components of the simplest reef-type aquarium, exemplified by the original Dutch minireef. They are **increased illumination**, an **open top** and **surface overflow**, and the **dry-wet filter**. Of these, only the last two are new since multiple fluorescents and spot-lights or mercury lamps have already been used with natural system and other tanks. In fact, the miniature reef is an elaboration of the natural system, using various ways of increasing its efficiency.

The Dutch Minireef

In this design, the importance of making the best use of the illumination provided and of maximizing the gas exchange at the surface of the water is catered to by omitting the usual cover glasses and placing the fluorescent tubes close to the surface of the water. They rest on glass strips and a glass or plastic container at the back of the tank holds the starters and ballasts. All are rendered as waterproof as possible, but still have the potential for splash or salt creep to reach them. As all of this is under a hood, an air pump to remove

heat and to agitate the surface of the water is added.

Two partitions are placed so as to cut off one back corner of the aquarium. The first is close to the corner and provides a dry vertical prismatic tube down which electric wiring and a hose are passed, the latter to return filtered water from the pump in the dry-wet filter. (This feature could well be omitted and the wiring and hose left external to the tank.) The second is a larger partition cutting off another trapezoidal area that will receive water from the surface of the aquarium, filter it, and pass it on to the dry-wet filter situated below the aquarium via a tube running from a hole in the bottom of the tank. This partition has its top a little below the first with a series of shallow slots to keep the overflowing water surface at a safe level. Various filtration media may be used in this overflow, the simplest being a spiral of filter padding to catch any gross particulate matter, to be removed as necessary. Living rock has been used, but a filter pad should be placed on top of it for the same purpose.

It would seem best to keep this pre-filter as simple and as well oxygenated as possible so as to deliver water to the dry-wet filter as near to saturated as can be achieved. Smit states that a biological filter, dry-wet or undergravel, cannot be supported unless the oxygen level is above 5.8 mg (per liter). If this is so, we are working very near to the limit, as sea water at 77°F (25°C) can only hold 6.86 mg per liter, and so must be 85% saturated for the dry-wet filter to work. You may recall from Chapter 1 that at 77°F, a liter of sea water holds only 4.8 ml of oxygen, or 6.86 mg approximately.

The agitation of the water surface plus skimming it into the pre-filter prevents the formation of a film of proteinaceous, fatty or other matter that accumulates at the surface of an ordinary aquarium. This, together with free access to fresh air, means that better light penetration and better oxygenation does in fact occur so that the water delivered to the filtering system is as well oxygenated as possible. It will

however be robbed of some of its oxygen by the wet portion of the dry-wet filter and so be delivered back to the aquarium less than fully saturated. To counteract this, it is returned back via the corner channel to the top of the tank and led into a spray bar placed over the surface towards the back. Oxygen dissolves very rapidly in water, whereas carbon dioxide (CO_2) leaves it rather slowly. The result is that the returning water is once more well oxygenated but it will still have a fair amount, undetermined, of CO_2 left in it. This will benefit plants and zooxanthellae and as long as there is not too much it will not seriously lower the pH.

If the minireef is also provided with a denitrifyer, a portion of the water from the pre-filter is diverted by a bleed-off valve into it and after passing through at a slow rate the water is then sent to join the rest in the dry-wet filter. It will be deoxygenated and must depend on the dry portion of the filter to regain oxygen. Fortunately, it only represents a small fraction of the circulating water. This does not seriously detract from the oxygenation of the system as a whole. Too big a fraction would do so. It is essential that denitrification be carried out on only a small proportion of the circulating water, as indeed its slow passage for the process to be effective demands.

The heater may be hidden in the aquarium itself. It is more easily regulated and replaced if it is in the pump section of the dry-

George Smit of Holland has been the "father" of the Dutch minireef. He has issued video cassettes covering the subject and has made some excellent photographs of thriving minireefs. The photograph below shows one of Smit's excellent photographs.

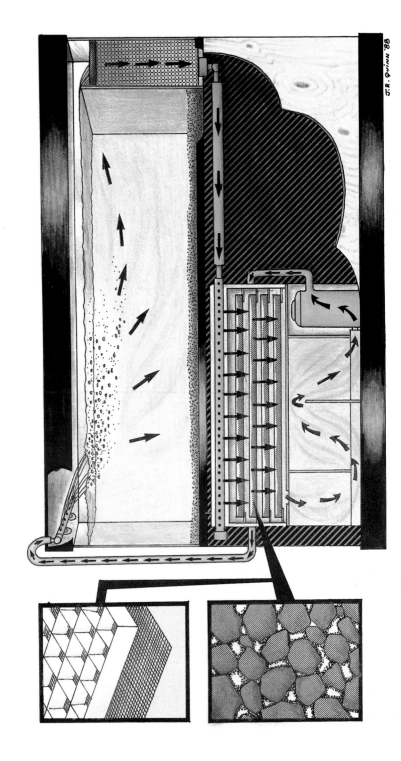

THE PRINCIPLES OF THE BIO-MECHANICAL MINIREEF FILTER
This schematic shows a typical minireef setup produced, for example, by the firm Oceanarium Products and Design,Inc. It features a dry-wet filter hidden in the aquarium stand. The four layers of dry filtering is accomplished with the use of a plastic grid similar to the light diffusers used in fluorescent lighting fixtures. Under the grid is a plastic screening with about a quarter-inch mesh. On top of this are Biobeads or similar bases for the establishment of nitrogen-fixing bacteria. The water overflows into a mechanical filter and drops by gravity into the dry-wet filter through a series of perforated water outlets on top of the dry-wet filter. The water drips through the four layers of filter material and accumulates in the bottom. It then passes through a maze and is pumped back into the aquarium, causing desirable water turbulence. Drawn by John R. Quinn.

wet filter. If so located, it will have to be of fairly high wattage because the sprinkler system by which the water is returned to the tank will cool it down quite a bit. Placed within a 60-70 gallon (230-270 liter) tank, a 150-watt heater is ample, but if in the filter, a 200-watt model would be safer. Of course, lower wattages will be sufficient in air-conditioned or heated premises. A brisk circulation rate is beneficial, up to 5 or 6 tank volumes per hour is not too much, and this in itself will tend to dissipate heat.

A minireef is usually housed in a neat cabinet, with a hood covering the top of the aquarium and hiding the works, but with good ventilation provided by an open back. The dry-wet filter sits in a compartment below the aquarium together with electrical outlets and any other equipment. If a protein skimmer is to be used it may present a minor problem to the aquarist wanting to keep visible equipment to a minimum. A really efficient model will have to be situated outside the cabinet, but sufficiently effective ones can go into the cabinet or even into the minireef. The latter is not usually regarded as desirable since the whole object of a "window on the sea" effect is defeated by visible apparatus of such a kind and it is not usually feasible to hide it behind the living rock. Some regard the skimmer as a temporary piece of equipment only, to be used for a few hours now and again and dismantled when not in use. This is probably the best solution as there is seldom need for its continuous use.

Keeping the water in the minireef moving is desirable. It brings the almost invisible food within reach of the stationary invertebrates, as well as reducuing temperature stratification. The ideal water movement is equal to 5.5 times the capacity of the tank every hour. Photo by George Smit.

The Minireef H-39

A recent modification of the minireef available for 30-100 gallon tanks (114-380 liters) keeps all the equipment on one level, indeed within the one aquarium. The lighting arrangement is as before, plus the open top and surface overflow, which runs into a heater chamber. From the heater chamber the water enters a protein skimmer and then into a spiral "dry" filter, called an *aerobic biological spiral filter*. From the spiral filter it is returned to the aquarium by a water pump (powerhead). This pump also sends part of the water through a

The Dutch garden minireef and other minireef aquariums are as much a garden as an aquarium. The living invertebrates are more beautiful and much more interesting than any aquatic garden. This is shown in the lovely photos of George Smit, one of which is above.

denitrifying (Denitra) filter whence it is returned to the spiral "dry" filter. All of this equipment is at one end, within the rectangular aquarium. Note that the "wet" filter is omitted. An air pump supplies the protein skimmer and is the only piece of equipment exterior to the set-up.

Other Systems

As the idea of the miniature reef is catching on, various other but essentially similar systems are being evolved. The Dupla system offers the basics of a minireef, adequate lighting plus "dry" filtration using the Dupla Bioballs already described. The lighting available includes mercury vapor and quartz iodide lamps that sit well above the aquarium because of the heat produced. Cable heating of the tank is also offered,

One of Lee Chin Eng's early experiments with a minireef using his "natural system." Living on the sea in Indonesia, Lee had access to unlimited water changes and living rock.

attached to the bottom of the aquarium and thus completely out of sight. Dupla offers a large range of high quality accessories that may be applied to any system and thus it is easy to convert an existing aquarium. Specialist petshops sell Dupla or similar equipment.

The conversion of aquaria already in use to the equivalent of a minireef is important to the average aquarist because of the cost of totally new equipment. People are beginning to build their own at a fraction of the cost of a fully commercially made set-up. Intelligently planned and used they work perfectly well. The first and essential steps must always be proper illumination and oxygenated (dry) filtration. Dry-wet filtration is probably better, while protein skimming and denitrification may help a lot depending on circumstances. The heavier the biological load and the less the dependence on plants, the greater the likely need for these additional measures. It seems unlikely that external algal filters will take on in the home aquarium despite their successful use in large establishments. They require too much attention, extra lighting and are liable to fail unless on a large scale with the possibilities of alternate routing of the water.

Filter Materials

The advantage of using synthetic materials such as

The centerpiece of this Dutch minireef is a pair of clownfish in a huge sea anemone. The living rock that surrounds the anemone has not blossomed yet as the setup is still new, but the landscaping will become more and more picturesque as the invertebrates grow. Photo by George Smit.

matting or Bioballs as a filter material instead of coral sand or the like is lightness. In a filter of coral sand much depends on the grain size. If, as a rough guess, we estimate this to average 2 mm, there will be a surface area per gallon of the order of 6 m² or 60 sq feet approx. If the average grain size is 4 mm, halve the above estimate of surface area, but it is still 3 m² or 30 sq ft. Both of these estimates are larger than the quoted area of Bioballs, that is

21.5 sq ft per gallon. I have seen no estimates for other materials, except that plastic matting has been stated to have a greater surface area than coral sand, but with no supporting evidence.

It seems that plastic filters probably do not differ greatly from coral sand in the area they offer to bacteria, so the immediate advantage remains their lightness. It is of interest that in a conventional undergravel filter covering the base of a tank, a much greater surface area is offered than in smaller external filters, where the advantage is of greater oxygenation. If 10% of the tank volume of Bioballs is used with a 60-gallon (230 liter) tank the volume of Bioballs, 6 gallons, will have a surface area of 129 sq ft as against an estimated 500 sq ft for the undergravel filter if this is 3″ (7½ cm) deep with 2 mm grain size, or 250 sq ft with a 4 mm grain size. Forgive the mixed measuring systems, but it would be tedious to give both in all examples. The tank bottom is estimated at 120 × 40 cm (4 × 1⅓ ft).

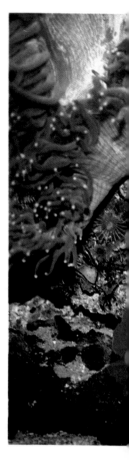

However, the external plastic filter, particularly Bioballs or the spiral filter, has not only the further advantage of availability but also of durability, needing infrequent attention or even none at all for a very long period. As long as the surface area is adequate it does not matter that another filter can offer more because it would not be fully utilized anyway. The bacteria grow to whatever extent is needed, but no more, and excess surfaces are not utilized.

(How do I arrive at the figures for coral sand? Here goes! Imagine a liter of solid coral, absolutely solid, carved up into 2 mm cubes. A liter is 1000 cm^3 = 125,000 cubes each 2 mm per side. These will have a surface

The hobby of keeping a minireef is very enlightening. Not only must you master the techniques of salt water chemistry, but you have to know about invertebrates and fishes, and the relationship between them both. The only book(s) covering the subject have been written by Dr. Leon P. Zann under the titles LIVING TOGETHER IN THE SEA and THE MARINE COMMUNITY AQUARIUM. Books like these, and other pet books, are available at your local petshop.

area of 24 mm² per cube, or 25 × 125,000 mm² per liter, which equals 3,000,000 mm², or 3m² or 30 sq ft approx. This is 114 sq ft per gallon. However, the little cubes would not pack solid, perhaps 50% packing is as good a guess as any, so we estimate 57 sq ft per gallon - call it 60! I know, there are no cubes in coral sand, more like spheres, but you are welcome to do the corresponding calculation and find that the answer is much the same.)

There are further considerations. Dry-wet filters or just "dry" filters alone are not only better oxygenated but are more efficient than an undergravel filter, parts of which may be inactive due to poor design, clogging or the formation of channels passing the water through regions of low resistance. It is impossible to give figures for such eventualities. If the tank gets an overload of pollution, the oxygen content of the water may fall below that needed to keep the undergravel filter operating, and then we are in real trouble. There is less chance of it happening with a dry filter and sprinkler system.

So we have the following progression: natural system ◊ natural system plus undergravel filter ◊ natural system plus external dry-wet or dry filter (= minireef) ◊ miniature reef plus protein skimmer and/or denitrifyer. Each step is an improvement, or potentially so.

One of Lee Chin Eng's natural method aquaria . . . the first of the successful minireef techniques. Photo by Edgar Smith.

Chapter 4
SETTING UP AND MAINTENANCE

There are basically two ways of setting up a miniature reef aquarium. As with any system employing biological filtration, the filter must keep pace with the load of living material in the tank. It can do this either by artificial preparation before introducing the live creatures, or it can develop gradually with them as long as they are introduced gradually. There are grounds for preferring the first way, that will be explained later, but it is sometimes not possible to put everything, or at least most things, into the aquarium all at once, either because of availability or expense. The basis of the system, living rock, is itself expensive and the corals, anemones, etc., to be added are equally so. A large tank costs a lot of money to furnish and this may have to be accomplished gradually.

Living Rock

Living rock is old dead coral, usually compacted, that has been colonized by all kinds of invertebrates and may be some fishes as well. It will also carry algae of their spores and in nature is teeming with life. Different kinds of living rock carry quite different populations, some will be rich in algae, some in anemones or zooanthids and the like, some in soft corals, usually small ones, some in tube worms, crustaceans and even small hard corals. It pays to get as good a variety of

rock as possible so that a good mixed population is there from the start. It is also much the best to get living rock straight from the ocean to your aquarium if at all posssible as the more hands through which it passes the more it will lose. Try to get your petshop to order the rock for you and to keep it as it arrived and not to put it into his tanks before you get it from him. Even the water that drains from it should be placed in your tank since it will be full of life.

If the recommendation above is impossible, then a different procedure will have to be followed. Living rock is often shipped practically dry and on arrival, sometimes after several days, many of the creatures will be dead. The dealer then cures it by placing it in a tank with an undergravel or dry-wet filter, maybe shaking the dead creatures out of it as far as possible and syphoning them off, and then leaves it for a few days or a week or so until the pollution dies down. Now, much depleted of its goodies, the rock is ready for sale. It will recover slowly, not to the original splendor, but quite surprisingly. Spores will hatch, algae will grow, creatures will have survived in nooks and crannies and in a month or two, possibly even longer, the rock will appear full of life once more. Never with as varied a population as it once had, but still plenty to build upon.

Those familiar with the natural system will remark that this is exactly how it is started up. Quite so, for the miniature reef aquarium is in fact an improved natural system, as we saw in the last chapter.

You can, if you wish, build up a temperate water aquarium along the same lines. The living rock will be real rock and not coral. It will be more modestly populated with a variety of invertebrates. Algae, of course, will be added to from locally available species, many of which are brightly colored and attractive even from cold waters, particularly some of the anemones and crustaceans. I have seen very attractive aquaria built up along

One of John Burleson's lovely photographs of a thriving minireef featuring leather corals. Many aquarists report great success with these hardy corals.

these lines, the cost of furnishing them being almost nil!

Method 1 This method is to be adopted when you can obtain as much living rock as is required to fill the aquarium all at once. It will be built up into a reef-like structure sloping from near to the top back to near to the bottom front.

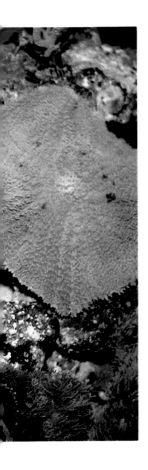

Particularly in a large tank, it is a good idea to give the living rock a base of cured dead coral so that precious live material is not wasted by being buried underneath other rock. If it is, much of it will die off and cause pollution in the tank. Use open dead coral as much as possible so that a circulation of water under the "reef" is possible and light-avoiding sponges and other invertebrates may populate it.

If the aquarium were filled with living rock as above, particularly with fresh living rock, and the filter was newly set up without conditioning, there would be a risk of generating a smelly mess, with a die-off of some of the rock and a rapid rise in ammonia production. It might not happen, since living rock contains a lot of nitrifying bacteria, but if corals and anemones and other living invertebrates were added as well, it certainly would! So the filter must be preconditioned before anything else is attempted. The same method is used as for an undergravel filter in an old-style aquarium.

The bacteria concerned in nitrification are slow-growing in comparison with the general run of bacteria and so the process of conditioning can never be quick. By the older methods of putting a few tough fishes or turtles into the tank and gradually building up the population from there, it takes a month or more. Conditioning with pieces of dead fish or meat is no quicker, merely smellier. The most rapid and effective way is to use the ammonia they would be producing as a pure compound, first seeding the filter with some coral sand from another conditioned tank or with a culture obtainable from your aquarium shop.

If the set-up of your aquarium allows it, there is no need to circulate the water through the whole system while conditioning the filter, just circulate it through the filter system. If not, you will have to put the whole equipment into action and fill the tank as well, therefore using more of the ammonium salt. The essential thing is to use enough of the salt, ammonium chloride is best, to condition the filter to as high a capacity as you expect from it. Whatever dosage you use, you will get an ammonia peak followed by a nitrite peak so the occurrence of these is no guarantee that the filter has been fully conditioned. There is a formula for determining how much ammonium chloride to use but it is complicated. A rule has therefore been devised to cover the highest likely requirement of the aquarium, based on reasonable assumptions about how heavily it will be stocked.

Make up a 10% solution of ammonium chloride and add 2 ml for every 25 gallons (100 liters) of circulating water on each of the first two days, then add an extra 2 ml per day on days 3 and 4, a further 2 ml on days 5 and 6 and so on until 10 ml per 25 gallons per day is reached. This will take 10 days. Continue with 10 ml per 25 gallons per day until the nitrite peak has passed and the nitrite level is less than 0.5 ppm. You may wish to follow the development of the ammonia and nitrite peaks and to take daily measurements out of interest, but it isn't necessary to do so. It is sufficient to start measuring just the nitrite levels from about day 10 on unless you have added a lot of starter culture or old sand, when it could occur earlier, but it usually won't. Don't be fooled if you start early and get a low nitrite reading; it probably hasn't started to rise yet, so continue for a week or so to be sure of what is happening. A peak of 10 or 20 ppm is to be expected.

This method of conditioning the filter gives it a much greater capacity to handle ammonia than it would otherwise develop. By supplying ammonia from the start, the growth of *Nitrosomonas* and *Nitrobacter* is encouraged. They compete more successfully with other bacteria and so a larger final culture is achieved. Some claim a 300% improvement, even though most authors recommend lower amounts of ammonium chloride than I do. When you are ready to fill the aquarium, continue to treat the filter with 10 ml per 25 gallons

Thirty years ago, this is what a typical marine aquarium looked like. Bleached coral, plastic plants and few fish. Photo by Earl Kennedy.

per day if the filter alone has been receiving the treatment. Then fill the main tank with a high grade synthetic sea water. Make sure that the tap water used in making it up has been treated for chloramines with a commercial preparation or with 1 grain per gallon (65 mg per 4 liters) of sodium thiosulphate (photographer's "hypo"). Chlorine alone will blow off within a few hours and needs no treatment. Connect the filter to the tank and get everything working as it should, keeping up the ammonium chloride at the same rate per 25 gallons of total water. Then stop the ammonium chloride treatment and within a day or two, not more,

build up the miniature reef, even adding a few extra invertebrates, corals, anemones or such, if you like. The filter can take care of them. If you wait too long the filter capacity will decline and more care would have to be taken. If the tank has been included in the circulation from the start, simply stop the ammonium chloride, change as much of the water as you can manage to reduce the nitrate level, at least 50% if corals are to go in soon, and next day put in the reef, etc. Always remember that a biological filter is not static and that it adjusts rather slowly to changes in the biological load (biomass). If the biomass decreases, the filter loses capacity and needs time to build it up again. Changes upwards must always be slow after the initial balance has been struck.

Method 2 If the reef is to be built up gradually there is no point in fully conditioning the filter since it will only lose capacity if, to begin with, the biomass is small. In this case, there is no need to treat the filter beyond seeding it with the necessary bacteria. Without the seeding, they would eventually develop but would take a long time to do so. If just a few small pieces of living rock are put in at any one time, the filter will keep pace with them. It is still wise to check that this is happening by taking periodic ammonia and nitrite readings, particularly the latter. There should be no peaks beyond perhaps small initial ones. If a fair amount of living rock is introduced as a start, although more will be added, condition the filter with one half or one third of the amounts recommended earlier and look for earlier peaks and an earlier building of the reef.

Using Method 2, invertebrates can be added gradually, along with the living rock, together with some macro-algae such as *Caulerpa, Halimeda* and *Penicillus*. For best results, still use some dead coral as a base so that light-loving specimens can be placed as near to the top as possible. Keep an eye on the overall development of the reef, as it becomes less and less desirable to rearrange things once they have settled down. Try for a good color mix of as many types of invertebrates as your tank can hold, but keep an eye also on compatibility. The eventual amount of living rock can reach the commonly recommended 2 lbs per gallon (1 kg per 4 liters) or even more, but this is not mandatory. In some ways, it is better to have an **underpopulated** tank than an overpopulated one, although it is hard to overpopulate a miniature reef system as far as the filter capacity is concerned. Room must be left for growth and proper display.

This aquarium in Nancy, France supports a few anemones and clown (anemone) fishes. Unfortunately it has been taken over by filamentous algae that has choked off growth of the living rock. Photo by Dr. Denis Terver.

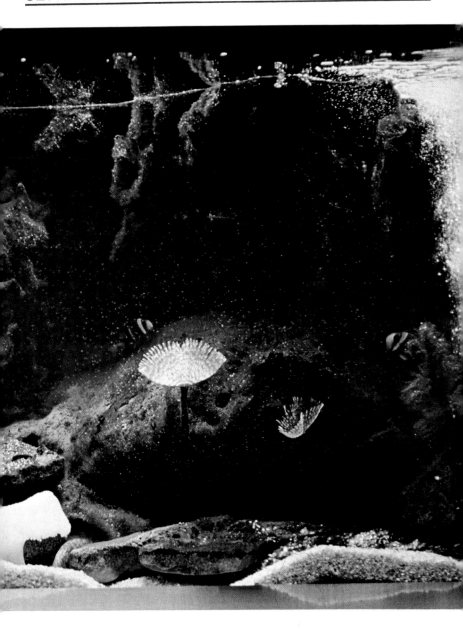

Building the Reef

We have already seen that the reef should, when fully developed, reach from near top back to near front bottom of the aquarium. There should not be more than ¼-½" (½-1 cm) of coral sand on the bottom since there is no undergravel filter and we don't want areas of anaerobic bacteria inside the tank, turning the sand gray and giving rise to noxious gases. As the reef is built up, make sure that it has platforms and niches that will accept additions of corals, anemones and other invertebrates and give shelter to the mobile ones like shrimps and fishes. The higher the quality of the rock and the less it has lost before you get it, the more it will need attention. Some specimens of rock will harbor noxious creatures that must be eliminated as far as is possible.

The reef will always need some attention but less than that needed in the first few months. If possible, take photographs of the reef at intervals to remind yourself what it looked like at various stages and you may be surprised! Most reefs go through a lot of development, rather like a newly growing forest, until eventually, also like a forest, they reach a steady or near-steady state that may take a year or two to occur. A forest takes centuries!

Things to get rid of as far as you can in the early stages are crabs, predatory slugs, starfishes and other critters that destroy the scenery and feed on the very invertebrates you wish to cultivate. These will develop from larvae at first undetected but that grow up fast. Not all crabs or starfishes are unwanted. You must watch the behavior of those that turn up and get rid of predators. Some unwanted invertebrates feed on algae and these too must go. There are pretty little green slugs of various species that feed on *Caulerpa* and are very hard to see, but left to proliferate will devastate your *Caulerpa*.

There is also the question of unwanted algae, usually hair algae and encrusting or enveloping types, green, brown or red, often purplish. Once a tank has a preponderance of macro-algae these are often kept in abeyance, but they have a habit of

cropping up early and becoming a considerable nuisance. It is often the case that brown or red algae develop first in an aquarium and it is usually stated that this is due to insufficient light. It may be, and when green algae take over the others often disappear, but not always! Increasing the light intensity, that is good anyway in a miniature reef tank, can be accompanied by an even more luxurious growth of some all-enveloping red types that threaten to smother pretty well everything if they are not frequently removed by hand or syphoning. Eventually they disappear, but may take their time.

The lesson in all this is to introduce some macro-algae early on, cultivate it as much as possible and get to a stage where it needs frequent cropping to keep it in check. *Caulerpa* is the best to start with because it grows rapidly from cuttings - most algae don't - and offers a beautiful variety of species. Other species of higher algae need to be introduced attached to pieces of rock or coral and usually do best at a later stage of development. More about them, and *Caulerpa*, in the next chapter.

There are many types of miniature reef. If you look around for them or study photographs in

Another of the tanks in the famous aquarium in Nancy, France. These huge tanks feature a small number of fishes and excess light causing uncontrollable algae of the wrong varieties. Instead of dead, bleached corals can you imagine how beautiful this tank could be with living rocks? Photo by Dr. Denis Terver.

hobbyist books and magazines you will know what I mean. Some abound in algae, some are virtually or even completely devoid of them. Some have mostly coral, some mostly anemones and the like, and the mixtures of other invertebrates they carry can be very different. Some have fishes, some do not, but most people seem to find that at least a few give movement to the tank and make for greater interest. A general rule is to avoid having too many creatures other than filter feeders since to cater for them is difficult, except for fishes, that know to come and get it.

The extent to which algae are present, either as macro-algae or within the tissues of corals, etc., influence the desirability of equipment other than the dry-wet filter. Plenty of well-lit algae means that nitrates will be mopped up efficiently and the need for a denitrifyer is reduced. In fact, you can get along perfectly well without one, as does many a miniature reef. Algae do not remove much of the material disposed of by a protein skimmer and may even be contributing to it, so that a protein skimmer, although not essential, can still be an advantage. However, activated carbon may do as efficient a job, depending on circumstances. When fewer algae are maintained, even with plenty of algae-containing Cnidaria (coelenterates) that supply much

of the algal nitrogen, the advantage of using denitrifying equipment grows and a tank containing very few free-living algae will certainly benefit from it.

Despite accounts of zero nitrate in miniature reefs, some form of usable nitrogen must be present for algae to grow. Natural sea water contains up to 5 or 6 ppm of dissolved organic compounds, but only about 10% of these are simple ones like ammonia or nitrates. The rest are proteins, polypeptides, amino acids and vitamins. So around 0.5 ppm of simple nitrogenous compounds is enough for algal growth, although maximum growth rates are seen in the laboratory with more like 50 ppm of substances like sodium nitrate. However, corals do not thrive in such concentrations of nitrate, nor even do larval fishes. One wonders what the concentration of free nitrogenous compounds is in the cells of corals and other algae-containing creatures and if their algae are perhaps bathed in quite a rich solution.

Water Quality

Those with the most experience of the miniature reef systems insist that water changes are not only unnecessary, but positively not desirable. Evaporation is quite high because of the open tank and sprinkler systems and must be made up by the addition of fresh water at frequent intervals since

In the 1950's this was a successful aquarium. Lots of fish, lots of color and the only thing living were the fishes! Tanks like this are still possible for people who don't want to start a minireef aquarium. Photo by Dr. Herbert R. Axelrod.

the salts do not evaporate. There will be some loss from splash and salt creep - the bane of the marine aquarist. So a check must be kept on the specific gravity of the water and some additional salt mix added when necessary. Corals do not like much dilution, so it is advisable to keep the specific gravity around 1.022 at 78°-80°F (26°-27°C), which is equivalent to full strength sea water at 60°F (15°C), when the specific gravity is 1.025.

It is hard to believe that the composition of unreplaced salt water in a miniature reef aquarium does not change significantly, but I have seen no analyses. If corals grow, calcium must come from somewhere. It may in part come from the living rock and coral sand but this is dubious at the pH of a marine tank, and many aquarists choose to add it in the form of calcium salts from time to time, often with other minerals, vitamins and nutrients. The amounts vary enormously, from a tablespoon every other day to a teaspoon fortnightly, and so does the nature of the calcium added. In my own aquaria with flourishing corals, I add nothing, but I ignore the experts and make water changes with real sea water, about 10% per month. Away from the sea, I would add some powdered calcium carbonate or sulphate (blackboard chalk), about a teaspoon per month; it can do no harm added to the filter and you

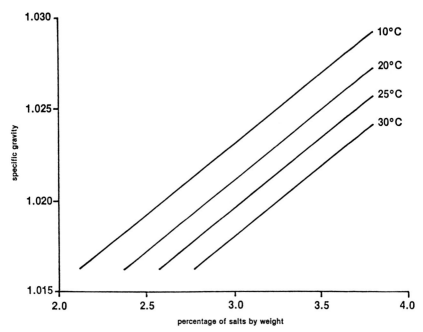

The relationship between specific gravity and salinity (percentage of salt) at different temperatures. After a chart in the book THE MARINE AQUARIUM IN THEORY AND PRACTICE by Dr. C. W. Emmens. This book is available at every petshop selling marine fishes.

can see if it accumulates or disappears. Algae manufacture vitamins, but again the addition of a small amount of trace elements and vitamins as supplied commercially would be O.K. Different algae require different trace elements so a good mixture is indicated. The calcareous algae also require a lot of calcium.

Naturally, a check on pH, specific gravity and nitrate concentration should be made fairly often, once every week of two at least, just to be sure of things. Why not ammonia and nitrite? Because, after the first peaks have passed and unless

some disaster happens, they will stay at zero or very near to it. But if you suspect that things are not as they should be, check the ammonia and nitrite levels without delay and if either is detectable, stop feeding and look very thoroughly for any cause such as dead material or filter trouble.

Some aquarists are very meticulous about water measurements. They measure the level of iron (needed by algae), of carbonate hardness and perhaps various other attributes. Some recommend very frequent and very small water changes, from 0.1% per day to 1 or 2% per week, which seems very tedious, but at least it keeps things turning over. I have not gone into such details because they are clearly not needed for success with the majority of miniature reefs, although they may help to guarantee it. Similarly, some aquarists believe in a very detailed

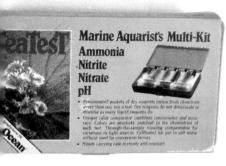

Marine Aquarist's Multi-Kit
Ammonia
Nitrite
Nitrate
pH

One of the great products produced to assist marine hobbyists is the Marine Aquarists Multi-Kit which contains the necessary reagents for testing for ammonia, nitrates, nitrites, and pH (acidity or alkalinity).

preparation of the living rock that removes most of its surface life. This results in a cleaner start but a long period of recovery during which lighting is only slowly introduced. Perhaps there is a 3-month interval before much happens and further life can be added. Once again, the advantage of this seems to be minimal.

If necessary, pH can be maintained by the addition of sodium bicarbonate, ½ teaspoon per 25 gallons (100 liters), with checks at each addition until the desired value is reached. Normally I would advise adding that amount each week to maintain the buffer capacity, but with no water changes it could lead to a sodium build-up.

While discussing water, it should be noted that the fluorescent lighting and various wires very near to the water surface are subject to salt corrosion. In a well-made system they will be rendered as water-proof and salt-proof as possible, but they will always need periodic cleaning. It is best to remove ballasts from above the tank to a safer position if at all possible. Electricity and salt water can be a lethal combination! For reasons that I have never fathomed, aquarium manufacturers like to place the ballast and starters beside the fluorescents. Yet in ordinary domestic ceiling lighting, they are placed above the fluorescents, a practice that has the advantage of allowing more tubes per surface area and of removing some of the heat, as well as some of the danger.

Feeding

A healthy miniature reef will produce quite a lot of its own food, both animal and vegetable. Many - preferably most - of the inhabitants will be filter feeders and zooxanthellae feeders, often both as in the corals and some anemones. Adequate lighting can support many such invertebrates, but a supplement of invertebrate

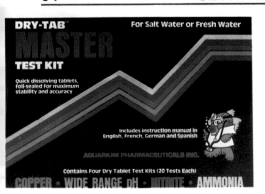

Master Test Kits combine nitrite, ammonia, copper, and pH test kits in a single package.

food two or three times a week will help, and is needed by those creatures not possessing algae. Follow the directions given by the manufacturer. They usually amount to around one drop per gallon at each feeding. As time goes on, you can judge for yourself the needs of your particular aquarium more accurately and adjust things accordingly.

In addition to invertebrate food, as sold commercially, newly hatched brine shrimp may, with advantage, be fed once or twice a week. They will benefit the corals and other filter feeders and remain alive until eaten. Shelled brine shrimp eggs may also be fed, and can be put straight into the aquarium. It is a matter of indifference whether they are consumed before hatching or afterwards; in fact the unhatched egg will be somewhat more nutritious than one that has lost

the energy used up in hatching. Used straight from the vial in which they are sold, one drop per gallon will supply around 1,500 eggs per drop.

Corals feed in practically every way possible, by absorbing the products of their zooxanthellae, by the direct absorption of organic compounds from the surrounding water, by the mucus absorption of small particles or the tentacular capture of larger ones, and finally by the capture of plankton and, in some cases, even of small fishes. They are really well adapted to their environment and in the case of the reef-building corals they switch from one technique to

USING BRINE SHRIMP. 1. Brine shrimp eggs, nauplii, and adults. 2. Petshops sell the necessary salt, pump, and eggs from which to hatch your own live food when you need it. 3. Add salt, water, and eggs. 4. Wait a day or more for the eggs to hatch. 5. Take out the airstone and net the brine shrimp. 6. Wash them under fresh water. 7. Feed them directly to the minireef aquarium. 8. You can grow them to adult size in a large tank, in the sunlight, with a little brewers yeast. Your petshop has all the details. Drawn by John R. Quinn.

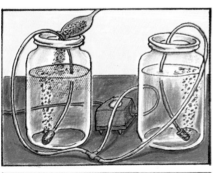

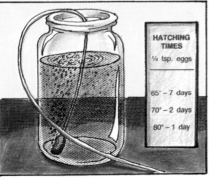

HATCHING
TIMES
¼ tsp. eggs

65° – 7 days

70° – 2 days

80° – 1 day

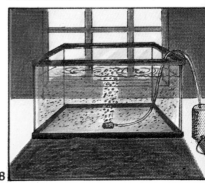

another as the opportunity presents itself by day and by night.

When feeding filter feeders it may be helpful to turn off the aquarium filters for a short period, say 10 to 20 minutes, so as to leave the food in the tank instead of removing most of it too promptly. However, except in the case of living food like newly hatched brine shrimp, the techique does have the disadvantage of ceasing to bring the food to the invertebrates by the currents in the water. An airstone turned on during the time when the filtration is off may be the best solution if arrangements are such that it causes no difficulties, such as unwanted splash.

Some of the larger anemones will benefit from occasional feedings of clam, shrimp or even meat or chicken. Just offer suitable sized chunks that they can ingest quickly and not reject half-digested at a later stage. Offer them on the end of a probe and stimulate acceptance by brushing the food against the tentacles. Later, many an anemone will accept the food if you just thrust it into its mouth; that helps to prevent the larger shrimps or crabs from getting it instead.

When fishes are introduced some will feed happily on the contents of the aquarium, particularly the omnivores that eat practically anything. Those that are purely vegetarian will not usually have been included as they would be too destructive. Many small fishes and the young of others are plankton feeders and will share in the newly hatched brine shrimp or shelled eggs when they are fed to the community. However, we must feed the fishes from time to time as most will not find enough from the living rock, or if they do, they would be cropping excessivly. How much to feed to fishes in a miniature reef tank is subject to debate. Some recommend as frequent and heavy a feeding routine as is usually practiced in an ordinary tank, others do not. Remembering that we have chosen fishes that will not damage the scenery too much, it is clear that they need regular feeding, but this should not be excessive. Fishes are very good at utilizing food, much better than we are, and if introduced when young they need not be fed as liberally as is needed to induce a maximum growth rate. After all, we do not wish to overcrowd the tank with large fishes.

Consequently, a light feeding once per day is felt to be adequate, preferably on live food

Under magnification of about 15 times actual size, live adult brine shrimp look like this. The San Fransisco Brine Shrimp Co. harvests and ships live brine shrimp like this all over the world. Petshops also sell brine shrimp eggs and both frozen and freeze-dried brine shrimp.

or frozen food, but flakes and pellets may be used too. In a natural system aquarium, feeding is even lighter - two or three times a week at most, but that is because the plankton is not filtered off as it is in the miniature reef tank. The dry-wet filter is capable of dealing with normal feeding if you decide to adhere to it, but it is felt that since fishes do not suffer hardship from a restricted diet (restricted within reason, of course) but merely regulate their growth to accommodate it, there is no point in encouraging high growth rates that will result in some of the fishes having to be removed at a later stage. In any case feed a variety of dry foods from different manufacturers. Petshops sell many different brands.

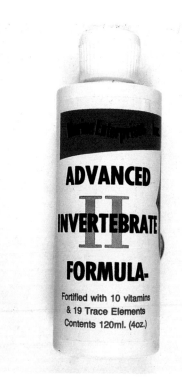

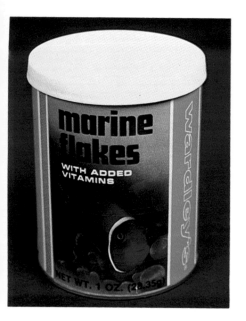

The rapid advancement of the popularity of minireef aquaria could only have been successful with the development of sophisticated products to keep invertebrates from starving to death. Petshops specializing in marine fishes welcomed products such as the Advanced Invertebrate formula to assist in invertebrate culture.

Specialty foods for marine fishes has been another remarkable development. Beware of those foods that claim they never cloud the water. Regardless of these claims, uneaten foods cloud aquarium water. NEVER overfeed your fishes. Fishes starving to death is almost an impossibility. Overfeeding, on the other hand, is almost a probability.

Chapter 5
THE LIVING REEF

Algae

Algae are remarkable in that they are placed into many divisions as different from one another in basic plans as are the phyla of the animal kingdom. They are more ancient than Animalia and have had longer to develop along different pathways. The macro-algae that we especially want to cultivate are divided into three main groups: green, red and brown. The green algae, of course, have chlorophyll and nearly always look green. The red and brown algae also have chlorophyll, but the various other pigments mask it and so they may appear almost any color, particularly the reds.

Green Algae (Chlorophyta) have alternation of generations, which means that a *sporophyte* generation, the usual seaweed described in the textbooks, produces spores that give rise to the *gametophyte* generation that produces reproductive cells, the gametes. This generation may or may not look like the sporophyte generation and so if a particular alga reproduces in the aquarium you may not recognize its offspring, only its grandchildren if they ever appear. The sporophyte is diploid, with two sets of chromosomes and the gametophyte is haploid and usually produces flagellated gametes (sex cells) like spermatozoa that may be equal or unequal in size and must meet and fuse to form the sporophyte.

The genus *Caulerpa* is a very popular green alga, possessing many different looking species but all with the rather rare property of growing from cuttings or fragments. Most of the other aquarium species do not reproduce in this way although they belong to the same family, the Caulerpaceae. *C. prolifera* has flat green fronds (thalli) with a branching holdfast that attaches to coral, rocks or the substrate. There are several fern-like species with a divided thallus, *C. mexicana, C. lanuginosa* and *C. crassifolia* are examples. *C. racemosa* and *C. peltata* have rounded knobs on divided branches; *C. cupressoides* looks like a long cactus; *C. verticillata* like a shaving brush; and so on.

Most other members of the family, that do not reproduce from fragments, include various amounts of calcium in their tissues. They should be acquired attached by their holdfasts to a piece of rock or coral so that they will thrive and grow. Species of *Halimeda* are like cacti, with calcified segments joined by flexible connections. *H. discordea* (baby bows) is a favorite, with circular green plates. Species of *Udotea* (green sea fans) look like their common name, with flat plates of calcified filaments. Species of *Penicillus* (Neptune's shaving brushes) have a tuft of free filaments on the end of a stalk, while *Rhipocephalus* species may resemble them.

Some of these species may appear spontaneously, and when they do it is an indication that the calcium status of the aquarium is satisfactory.

The family Ulvaceae (sea lettuce) provides the familiar algae

Minireef development will soon be applied to cold water aquariums. Great advances have been made in keeping cold water fishes. This aquarium received too much light stimulating the growth of filamentous algae. There are cold water anemones and other invertebrates.

of that name, *Ulva* and *Monostroma,* and hair algae of many genera and species. The family Dasycladaceae has many attractive species, particularly *Cymopolia barbarta,* like strings of beads with tufts at the tip.

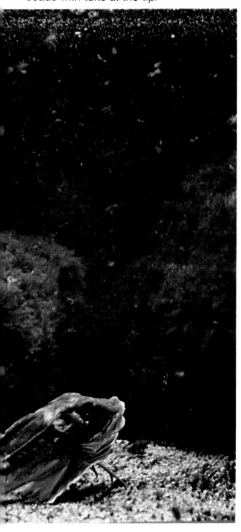

Brown algae (Phaeophyta) often have very complex life cycles, some resembling that of the green algae, others with the gametophyte generation parasitic, as it were, on the sporophyte. Eggs are retained in organs called conceptacles on the thallus and are fertilized by sperms also produced on a thallus - rather like advanced plants and animals. When gametophytes are free-living, they are usually tiny, but in some species both generations look alike.

Other than those that may appear spontaneously on living rock, brown algae are liable to cause trouble in the aquarium. They are too often likely to die off and give rise to toxic slime and color the water. The family Ectocarpaceae contains many hair algae that tend to smother other species, but some of the calcareous brown algae are safe and attractive. The family Dictyotaceae contains *Dictyota* and *Dilophus,* like branching, tough brown *Ulvas,* and *Padina* like little calcified fans.

Red algae (Rhodophyta) mostly have three generations and often don't appear red at all. Sporophyte and gametophyte generations usually look alike and are accompanied by a carposporophyte generation that stays attached to the gametophyte. The sporophyte produces sessile (non-motile) spores that grow into male and female plants that in turn produce sessile sex cells. The male cells are set free and act rather like the pollen of higher plants. From this union is produced the carposporophyte generation, parasitic on the female plant. This produces carpospores that grow into sporophytes. Contrary to the general rule, some red algae have tiny sporophytes and large gametophytes.

The red algae are usually small and suitable for the aquarium, flourishing in relatively poor light and not likely to foul the water like the brown algae. Red hair algae may, however, grow in shallow areas and cover rocks; *Bangia* and *Polysyphonia* species are examples. A deeper water and attractive, fern-like plant is *Laurencia,* with a number of species. Various calcareous red algae are familiar on living rock, forming pink or other colored encrustations. These are the corallines, larger members of which, but still quite small, are seen as jointed, hard and branching specimens, all in the family Corallinaceae.

This minireef aquarium is truly an underwater garden. It contains almost an unreal amount of color. The fishes are almost unnecessary in a setup like this one. Photo by John Burleson.

Cnidaria

Usually known as coelenterates, this phylum of the animal kingdom includes creatures built with a radial symmetry, a single mouth and no anus, possessing stinging cells called nematocysts. They are the anemones, corals, zooanthids and a host of similar beings.

The main anemones with which anemone fishes associate in nature are the *stichodactyline* group, with zoochlorellae (green indwelling algae) or zooxanthellae (yellow-brown indwelling algae). They feed on algal products, on prey caught with their tentacles or on food supplied by their fishy companions in some cases. The genera *Radianthus*, with long

variously colored tentacles, *Stoichactis,* with shorter, towelling-like tentacles and *Discosoma,* also short tentacled and often with green zoochlorellae are all "carpet" anemones, so-called because of their large potential size. *Tealia* species, usually with a red column below the tentacles, may be classed with the above, being large and favored by the anemone fishes as well. All require strong lighting to thrive.

Read any good book about marine invertebrates and you will find the very many genera of anemones that may be kept, some of which will reproduce in the aquarium. This they do by splitting into two or by budding off young from segments of the foot. They also reproduce sexually, and in some species the young develop in the central cavity and are finally ejected by the parent. Mushroom or elephant ear "anemones" (the corallimorphs) are favorites in the miniature reef aquarium, coming in almost any color and belonging to the genera *Actinodiscus* and *Rhodactis,* among others. So also are the colonial anemones, separate animals that nevertheless occur in masses and present a very coral-like appearance, usually having indwelling algae as well. Anemones, like corals, belong to the class Anthozoa, which do not produce medusae (jellyfishes).

The two other cnidarian classes are the Hydrozoa and Scyphozoa, with alternation of generations, some of the polyps of which make good aquarium specimens and may contribute to the plankton from time to time by releasing their medusae. *Hydractinia* is a tiny example, often seen on the shells of mollusks or crabs, and quite attractive when the polyps are expanded. However, the great majority of cnidarians you will come across are in the class Anthozoa.

The octocorals are Anthozoa with eight tentacles and include the soft corals, gorgonians and sea pens. Many of these can be kept in the aquarium; many of the soft corals, often without indwelling algae, are happy with moderate light and may reproduce. The well-known red

John Burleson took this magnificent photograph of an underwater garden of invertebrates. It is universal in its appeal.

organ-pipe coral is a soft coral with a harder skeleton than most and with green polyps. Few of those available will be named by your dealer, just go for attractiveness and hope for the best! Mostly you will be successful. Given a choice, the genera *Sarcophyton, Heliopora,* and *Xenia* are usually rewarding, while the very attractrive *Dendronephthya* tend to fail. The gorgonians offer a plethora of

different shapes and colors and mostly do well as long as they remain free of algae that tend to suffocate them if allowed to do so. Many of them are composed of flat plates of branching coral that filter off plankton from suitable currents and should be placed so that they can do this. The sea pens are anchored, usually in deep water, by a special polyp buried in the sand or mud while the other polyps are on a plume or rachis sticking up like a feather.

Although they do quite well and contain no algae, they are rarely kept.

The zoantharians are Anthozoa with twelve or more tentacles and so easily told from the octocorals. They include the anemones, already discussed, the stony corals, the tube-dwelling cerianthids, the zoanthids (anemone-like polyps) and a few others. The stony corals nearly all contain algae and thus need good

This lovely anemone, Radianthus ritteri, *abounds in the Indonesian reefs where Dr. Herbert R. Axelrod photographed this specimen.*

This specimen of Fungia *was also collected and photographed by Dr. Axelrod in Indonesia. The islands making up Indonesia, both freshwater sources as well as reefs, contain more interesting aquarium fishes than any other single location.*

This soft coral, Sarcophyton, *is a common Indo-Pacific species suitable for the minireef. Photo by John Burleson.*

lighting. The "day" corals that open in the light are naturally favored and among them the genera *Euphyllia, Goniopora, Alveopora* and some of the genus *Galaxea* are to be commended. The *Goniopora,* with about 40 species, are aggressive, relatively tough corals that can reach out over a foot (30 cm) from their base to sting surrounding coelenterates, so take care!

Corals are often very difficult to identify, the more so because the same species often comes in a variety of colors. *Goniopora* may be brown, gray, greenish or near white. *Alveopora* may be all these plus pink or blueish, all in the same species. The solitary Fungiidae with genera *Fungia* and others rarely open in daylight, but some do, while the also solitary *Cynarina* looks attractive by day although it is not extruding its tentacles. Instead, a water-filled coral body, pink or brown, protrudes from the skeleton. A similar phenomenon is seen in the so-called grape or bubble corals, genus *Plerogyra,* that also show blown-up tissue by day and tentacles at night. Various species by *Lobophyllia* also open at night, but are, nevertheless, quite attractively colored by day.

The family Dendrophylliidae, genera *Dendrophyllia, Tubastrea* and *Balanophyllia,* are ahermatypic and very spectacular even though they are not usually open by day. They come from

A lovely corner of a minireef aquarium photographed by John Burleson.

caves or deep water and are yellow, red or orange in color. The flesh snows up very well by day and if they are kept in a shady spot they may open too.

The cerianthids are often called tube anemones, but they are different from anemones proper. The tube, rubbery in texture and buried in sand or wedged in a crevice, may be up to a foot (30 cm) long and from it emerges a pastel-colored mass of long trailing tentacles that are lethal!

They can kill any small, unprotected creature that blunders into them, even shrimps that normally crawl over anemones with impunity. They are not, therefore, for every aquarium.

The zoanthids are also not anemones, but look rather like them. They are often colonial but occur as solitary forms in some species. *Parazoanthus* and *Palythoa* are colonial and do well in the aquarium, while some zoanthids are peculiar in that they grow much larger in the miniature reef tank than is usually found in nature.

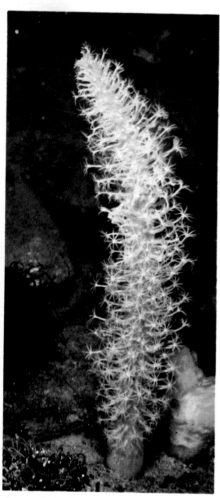

Cavernularia obesus, *the popular sea pen, opens up at night and enlarges. Sometimes these invertebrates are called sea feathers.*

During the day it closes up and looks rather inconspicuous. Photos by U. Erich Friese.

On the facing page is Goniastrea, *one of the staples for the minireef. Collected and photographed by Dr. Herbert R. Axelrod in Indonesia.*

Arthropoda

The species of this phylum number millions and include all animals with hard external skeletons and jointed limbs - insects, spiders, ticks, mites and crustaceans. The sea-dwelling crustaceans are what interests us. They are popular aquarium specimens, easy to keep for the most part, but caution must be exercised in choosing which of them to include in a miniature reef aquarium. Some are destructive and almost always regretted. Large crabs, lobsters and such are best avoided since they disturb the scenery, catch unwary creatures, including small fishes, steal food from anemones and grow rapidly even larger. They often emerge from living rock and gradually take over if not eliminated. Hermit crabs are more tolerable. If chosen when small they can be controlled by simply not providing them with large shells.

All crustaceans shed (moult)

This magnificent minireef was featured on the cover of the June 1988 issue of TROPICAL FISH HOBBYIST MAGAZINE. This magazine, affectionately known in the trade as TFH, has been a leader in popularizing marine aquariums and minireefs. Each issue contains several articles about the marine aquarium and the techniques for maintaining them. The magazine is available at most petshops. Photo by Dr. Denis Terver.

The arrow crab, Stenorhynchus seticornis, *appears in several color varieties.*

their integument (chitinous hard shell) at intervals to allow for growth. They do this even if no growth occurs. For obvious reasons growth can't occur without the inelastic coating being shed. At the same time, lost limbs or feelers are replaced, although it may take several moults for them to attain full size. When a moult occurs, the animal is at a severe disadvantage and must hide away until its new coat hardens; that may take a day or so. In the aquarium, with its crowded conditions, losses at this time will sometimes occur. The shed integument is so complete that a novice aquarist will wonder from where the new shrimp or whatever has come.

Shrimps are the most popular of the crustaceans. They don't grow too large nor are they aggressive. It must be remembered that many species live for less than a year. A nice exception is the genus *Stenopus* with a number of attractive species. The most common is *S. hispidus,* the banded coral shrimp. They are, however, quite aggressive, even towards other species of shrimp, and only mated pairs can be kept together. They are also cleaners, picking parasites from fishes that recognize them and hover over them to be serviced. In my own experience they are nowhere near as efficient as cleaner wrasses. A pair of *S. hispidus* is fascinating, going around together, the male feeding the female and each

Stenopus hispidus, the banded coral shrimp, is a very popular cleaner shrimp. Photo by Dr. Herbert R. Axelrod.

FACING PAGE: Alpheus lottiui, *the Seriatopora shrimp from the Indo-Pacific. Photo by U. Erich Friese.*
Bottom left: Lebbeus grandimanus. *Photo by T. E. Thompson.*
Bottom right: Gnathophyllum panamense *from Sonora, Mexico. Photo by Alex Kerstich.*

ABOVE: The coral is Galaxea fascicularis, *with a coral shrimp,* Rhynchocinetes. *Photo by Don Baker.*

guarding the other at moulting time.

Another cleaner shrimp genus is *Lysmata.* The red-striped *L. grabhami* is not aggressive and can be kept in groups. The genus *Periclimenes* also includes some cleaners, some commensuals that live with various other invertebrates such as anemones, sea cucumbers and sea urchins, and free-living species. *P. brevicarpalis* has small semi-transparent males, large well-colored females and lives on carpet anemones. The harlequin shrimps, genus *Hymenocerus,* are colorful and weirdly shaped. They feed in nature on the tube-feet of starfishes. In an aquarium without starfishes, they are said to adapt to other foods. The mantis shrimps (*Squilla* and other genera) are best avoided as they are

predatory and possessed of razor-sharp appendages that can slash your hand severely.

There are not too many desirable crabs. Many are nocturnal and rarely seen, others grow too large. However, some of the decorator crabs that cover themselves with algae, anemones, sponges, etc. are amusing and do not get too big. Various crabs that live with anemones, like *Porcellana,* are also interesting and harmless. The arrow crab, *Stenorhyncus seticornis,* is quite sizeable, with long legs and orange or red stripes, and also no trouble. Coral crabs, such as in the genus *Trapezia* can be brilliantly colored and small, living among the reef-building corals and matching their coloration.

The swarms of benthic and planktonic crustaceans that

LEFT: Stenopus cyanoscelis, *one of the cleaner shrimps from the Indo-Pacific. Photo by Ken Lucas in the Steinhart Aquarium, San Francisco, California.*

BELOW: The deadly mantis shrimp, Odontodactylus scyllarus. *These are omnivorous shrimp that eat everything, including anemones. They also trap live fishes. They should not be kept in the minireef aquarium. Photo by K. H. Choo.*

frequently inhabit marine aquaria must not be forgotten. They just appear from the living rock and from additions later on. Many are copepods, with pairs of eggsacs hanging from the females, some are amphipods, laterally flattened usually, but including the rather fascinating skeleton shrimp, *Caprella,* that loops along over seaweeds or hydroids. They are normally harmless and are eaten by various other invertebrates or by fishes but sometimes become

a nuisance. I am ignorning the
parasitic copepods like *Ergasilus*
that cause specific fish diseases
but will not normally emerge from
living rock.

ABOVE: This colorful crab, Lybia
*species, has two small anemones
which it brandishes to keep predators
at bay. Photo by Bruce Carlson.*

FACING PAGE: A cleaner shrimp,
Lysmata amboiensis, *cleaning a*
Chelmon rostratus.

Echinodermata

There are five classes of echinoderms: the **Crinoidea**, sea lilies and feather stars; the **Holothuroidea**, sea cucumbers; the **Echinoidea**, sea urchins; the **Asteroidea**, sea stars; and the **Ophiuroidea**, brittle stars. Looking very different from one another, all are built on the same plan of radial symmetry. A further characteristic of the phylum is a hydraulic system, the water vascular system, furnishing power to the tube feet.

The **Crinoidea** reached their maximum development millions of years ago as sea lilies, echinoderms like a feather star on a stalk. They are now practically confined to deep waters, but the free-living feather stars are still common, breaking free from the stalk they still have as juveniles. Many are colorful and attractive but break up readily and are subject to attack from fishes, crabs, etc. They are filter feeders and not difficult to keep if unmolested.

This type of minireef aquarium is easily within the reach of the average marine aquarist. It is not overcrowded with animals without backbones (invertebrates) and contains interesting, peaceful fishes.

Even small aquariums can be converted to a minireef setup. It only takes a few anemone fish, Amphiprion, *a suitable anemone, and a featherduster worm.*

The **Holothuroidea** swarm over many areas and may be debris feeders or filter feeders. They are mostly unattractive, long cylinders with a mouth at one end and an anus at the other, but a few are brightly colored, mainly in the family Dendrochirotida. These may be bright red or red, white and blue, with rings of large tentacles, rather difficult to feed and liable to extrude a toxin if things are not to their liking. On the whole, the sea cucumbers are to be avoided.

The **Echinoidea** are possessed of hard, calcified skeletons, spherical in shape except for the heart urchins. They travel around on their tube feet or by spines, long or short, that are characteristic of them. Another feature is the *pedicellaria,* little pincers on stalks that cover the body, keep it clean, capture small prey and convey it to the mouth.

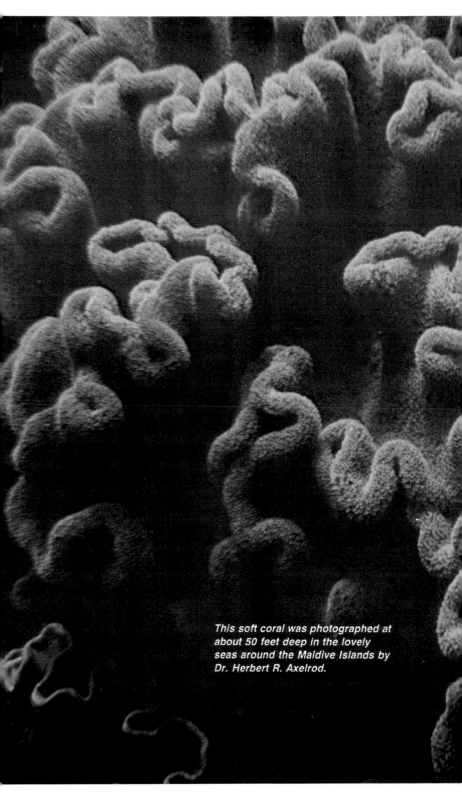

This soft coral was photographed at about 50 feet deep in the lovely seas around the Maldive Islands by Dr. Herbert R. Axelrod.

They can be debris feeders, algal or hydroid feeders or omnivores and wander all over the tank in search of food. Many tend to be nocturnal and so don't contribute much to the beauty of the aquarium. Some of the thick-spined urchins like *Heterocentrotus* or *Strongylocentrotus* are quite decorative. Some of the long-spined urchins are venomous, so beware.

The **Asteroidea** (starfish) are perhaps favorites among the echinoderms, but some do well while others do not. Others are a pest, consuming precious specimens and cleaning up living rock like a vacuum cleaner. Many a typical five-armed starfish attacks mollusks, pulling bivalves apart by a steady traction until the shell begins to open and then inserting its stomach to digest the victim. However, well-behaved specimens that do no damage and seem to live on nothing are included in the genera *Fromia* (mostly red), *Neoferdina* (yellow, mottled) and *Linkia* (*L. laevigata* is the well-known blue star). Yet

A sea urchin burrowing into a coral rock. Most burrowing sea urchins secrete a solvent that dissolves the rock as they burrow. Photo by M. Goto.

each star should be watched, just to be sure that it doesn't turn out to be a villain! Avoid the thick-bodied, chunky stars often on sale; they can extrude a toxic slime that kills off nearly everything.

The **Ophiuroidea** hide most of the time and are a bit of a loss. Most species are very liable to fragment as well. They are debris feeders, at least the smaller

LEFT: A red sea urchin, Strongylocentrotus franciscanus, *from the northeast Pacific Ocean. Photo by T. E. Thompson. RIGHT: Blue* Linckia *starfish are blue and found with a variable number of arms. Photo by Dr. Herbert R. Axelrod in the Fiji Islands.*

species are, but some of the large, tough genera such as *Ophiarachnella* are not only unlikely to break up, but are actively predatory. I had one large green specimen that regularly emerged at feeding time and competed with adult angels and other large fishes for chunks of clam that it seized in coiled arms. The penalty was frequently bitten-off arm tips, but that didn't deter it.

Annelida

The segmented worms, together with other worm phyla, will be present in your aquarium whether you wish it or not, mostly invisible and acting as scavengers and as food for some of the other inhabitants. Those of interest are the tube-building polychaetes that put out decorative crowns. There are others that could have a place but rarely do. Serpulids build limey tubes on rocks and coral from which they produce a head with a circle or circles of tentacles to collect food particles and small plankton. They come in various colors and sizes, with a crown that may reach as much as 5″ (12½ cm) across. Some, like *Pomatostegus,* have U-shaped crowns rather than circles. Sabellids build leathery tubes, but are otherwise very similar, both groups being known as fan or

The beautiful but dangerous stinging hydroid, Lytocarpus philippinus, *is not meant for the amateur minireef aquarist. Photo by Allan Power.*

feather-duster worms. The genus *Spirographis* produces corkscrew crowns up to 2" (5 cm) across, again in many colors. We can only assume that in many sea creatures, color is a matter of indifference and so there has been no selection against any particular hue.

The terebellid worms live in mucus-lined tubes and put out long tentacles that may scour for a foot (30 cm) around the entrance, picking up edibles and transferring them to the mouth. You may note their presence by these and never see the worm. The sea mice, genus *Aphrodita,* are fairly large, a typical free-living scavenging worms that tend to hide their beauty in the sediment or below cover. Much the size and shape of a mouse, when cleaned up they present quite a glittering and colorful appearance. Like some other polychaetes, they may sting when handled.

The parchment tubeworm, Chaetopterus, *removed from its tube. It probably cannot live long without its tube. Photo by Keith Gillett.*

FACING PAGE: Sabellastarte indica, the featherduster tubeworm. Photo by Walt Deas.

The ventral surface (underside) of a sea worm, Aphrodita. Photo by Alex Kerstitch. BELOW: Another sea worm, Hermodice carunculata. Photograph by Dwayne Reed.

Mollusca

The mollusks are vast in numbers, ranging from humble winkles to the quite intelligent octopus. They are soft-bodied animals that usually secrete a shell, have a muscular foot and typically a rasping tongue-like organ, the radula. Many will probably appear in the aquarium, growing up from the larvae or juvenile stages present in living rock. Most will be univalves, snail-like creatures.

Univalves have a head, usually a pair of eyes and crawl actively around in search of food. This is often algae, but the cone shells feed on other invertebrates; the whelks on other mollusks. The cone shells are dangerous to handle and have poisonous tips to the radulas. Limpets have a home base to which they return after feeding, fitting themselves into a depression in the rock that they have worn for themselves. The most commonly purchased univalves are cowries, genus *Cypraeae,* which have decorative shells covered much of the time by equally decorative mantles - a membranous part of the soft body. Despite their popularity, the feeding habits of cowries are poorly understood, but they get along in the marine aquarium.

Related to the univalves are many "slugs" that have little or no shell, the sea hares and nudibranchs. The sea hares, *Tethys* and other genera, are vegetarians and can survive in the aquarium, but nudibranchs are very specialized carnivores, each species feeding on particular sponges, corals, bryozoa, etc. Beautiful as they are, it is a pity to put them in a tank unless you can supply their needs, which is rarely the case, or are willing to watch a

Donax denticulata, *a coquina clam found in shifting sands. Photo by Charles Arneson.*

The poisonous cone shell Conus virgatus. *Photo by Alex Kerstitch.* BELOW:
Cyphoma signatum *feeds on gorgonians and might be an unwelcome guest in
your minireef aquarium. Photographed by David L. Ballantine in the Caribbean.*

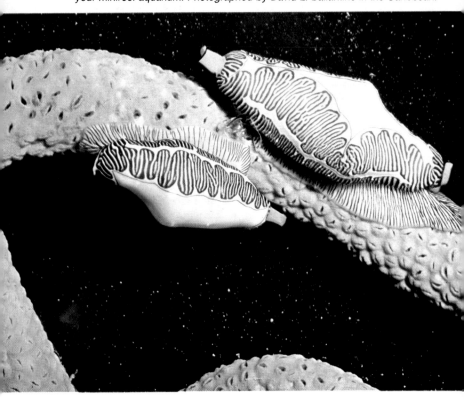

Cypraea rashleighana. *One snail has its mantle retracted, while the other has its mantle partially extended. Photo by Scott Johnson.*

fortuitously happy specimen feed on your favorite coral.

Bivalves secrete a hinged shell and are filter feeders. They include mussels, oysters, scallops and clams, the last two of which are frequently kept. Some clams such as the genus *Tridacna,* the giant clams, have indwelling algae and need good illumination, but most bivalves do not. Scallops are active creatures and can flap around by opening and shutting the shell or by expelling jets of water from around the hinges.

This is the real thing! A living reef taken about 20 feet depth in the Maldives Islands by Dr. Herbert R. Axelrod.

Lima, a popular genus, has red or pink flesh and long tentacles with usually a white shell.

The cephalopods, squids, cuttlefish and octopuses, seem far removed from their fellow mollusks; the octopus in particular is far more intelligent and can learn tricks in the laboratory. These are NOT creatures for the miniature reef tank as they are predatory, many are poisonous, most can foul the water with their ink and they are escapists par excellence. Even a large octopus can squeeze through an incredibly

FACING PAGE: The cuttlefish, Sepia, *is not meant for the minireef as it can spray black liquid (thus the name sepia) from time to time to detract predators. Photo by Pierre Laboute.*

A very interesting addition to the minireef is the sea scallop, Chlamys hericia. *This interesting animal is a swimming clam with lots of eyes glistening in the fleshy opening of the shell. Photo by T. E. Thompson.*

small gap and finish up on the
carpet, so what chance is there in
an open tank of keeping it in the
aquarium?

Other Phyla

Living rock will introduce all
kinds of curious creatures to the
tank, some will survive and
multiply, others will not. Various
encrusting sponges are common,
but few survive, yet it is not
unusual for one or two to appear
spontaneously and thrive for at

*BELOW: This is a living coral reef in
very shallow water in the Fiji Islands.
Photo by Dr. Herbert R. Axelrod.
RIGHT: Collecting living rock. This is
what the underside of a coral boulder
looks like when it is first collected.
Photo by Keith Gillett.*

least a time. They belong to the phylum Porifera and may be soft, calcareous or siliceous (with spicules) and are often brightly colored, red or yellow (*Cliona* species), violet (*Haliclona*), orange (*Hymeniacidon*), or, frequently, brown (*Extyodoryx,* etc.).

Beside the Annelida, already dealt with, half-a-dozen other phyla or worms will contribute their quotas. The Nemertea, or ribbon worms, are unsegmented, often quite large worms living under

LEFT: This Goniastrea *living rock was collected by Dr. Herbert R. Axelrod in 80 feet of water in Indonesia. It was transported back to Neptune, New Jersey, and has lived for years. This is a daytime photo when the* Goniastrea *was closed. Photo by Dr. Axelrod.*
BELOW: The sponge Haliclona rubens *is very common in the tropical Caribbean (not as far north as Bermuda). Photo by Dr. P. Colin.*

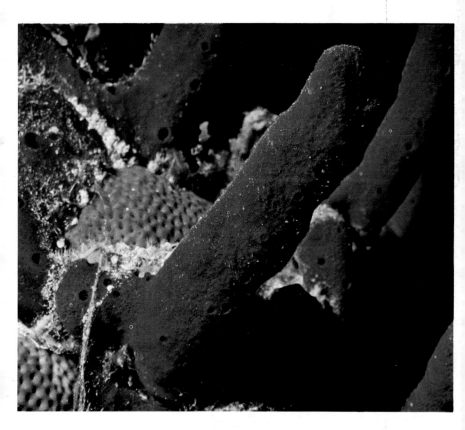

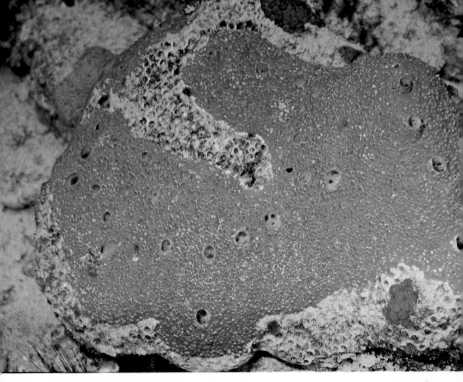

ABOVE: *The sponge* Toxadiocia *from California. Photo by D. Gotshall. TOP, LEFT:* Halichondria japonica, *the orange breadcrumb sponge, being carried on the back of a sponge crab,* Dromia dehaani. *Photo by Takemura and Suzuki. BOTTOM, LEFT:* Cliona delitrix, *a burrowing sponge encrusting the surface of its host coral, eventually killing it. Photo by Dr. Patrick I. Colin.*

rocks or rubble, usually dull in color but sometimes not. They are predatory and mostly invisible and so of little interest. The Platyhelminthes, or flat worms, sometimes contribute interesting free-living forms seen crawling over the rocks or glass, but are better known for the thousands of parasitic species many of which infest fishes. The Aschelminthes, roundworms, rotifers, etc., are also frequently parasitic, but the rotifers are getting attention as an important food for marine fish fry in attempts at breeding.

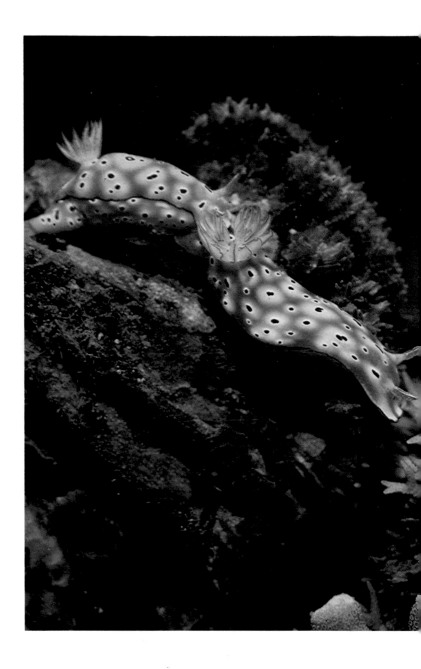

Chapter 6
FISHES

Fishes are best introduced several months after the miniature reef aquarium has become established. How many may eventually be kept depends on their size, habits and the nature of other living creatures present. The principles of the miniature reef aquarium may be applied with benefit to the keeping of fishes alone, but we are not thinking along those lines at the moment. With the characteristic inhabitants and plants of the living reef, we

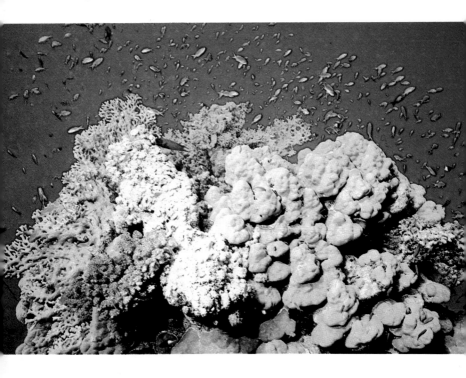

LEFT: Among the most beautiful creatures in the sea are the colorful snails without shells, the nudibranchs. The genus shown here is Ceratosoma. Photo by Allan Power. ABOVE: This beautiful coral head is Montastrea.

must avoid fishes that would be destructive, eating too much algae or any of our precious invertebrates or, indeed, smaller fishes. However, the early introduction of hair algae eaters may be a great help in tanks suffering from early infestation. This rules out, in general, surgeon

fishes (Acanthuridae), large angels (Pomacanthidae), chaetodons (Chaetodontidae) and many wrasses (Labridae). The surgeons eat algae, the large angels eat coral and various other invertebrates, so do chaetodons, and many wrasses love crabs and other crustaceans. Maybe you could put in a large wrasse early on to clean out unwanted crabs and later take him out and put in the crustaceans you wish to keep? Trigger fishes (Balistidae) are likely to be too much of a nuisance also, feeding on many types of invertebrates and also mostly

ABOVE: This branch coral is dangerous to touch. It is the stinging coral Millepora alcicornis. *FACING PAGE: Two corals predominate, namely* Acropora *species and* Mopsella ellisi. *Photo by Allan Power. These photos were taken in their natural habitat. It would take a huge aquarium of a thousand gallons to duplicate this scene.*

being very aggressive. Among the surgeons, the genus *Ctenochaetus* is cited as eating only hair algae and could be a useful addition instead of the usual disadvantage.

In a tank containing other small fishes, lion fishes (Scorpaenidae), groupers (Serranidae) and angler fishes (Antennariidae) would be a disaster, but they can be kept in a miniature reef aquarium perfectly well if with other large predators and if fed suitably. Similarly, sea horses and pipefishes (Syngnathidae) have a rather thin time of it if kept with other fishes since they do not feed quickly enough, but in the reef aquarium they can be kept on their own or with other slow feeders like mandarins (Callionymidae) and thrive. You can even mix them with small predators that cannot swallow them and have quite a unique collection, as the diets of the two groups do not conflict and neither feed on most of the reef creatures. Some of the predators might go for crustaceans however, but not for cleaner shrimps.

This leaves us with the question: what can we keep? The answer is, quite a list:

Dr. Gerald R. Allen took this serene photo of a living reef in Australia. The Spur Reef of the Great Barrier Reef is the exact location.

Pomacentridae - all of the
anemone fishes and practically
all of the damsel fishes.

Labridae - some of the smaller
wrasses like the cleaner
wrasse, *Labroides dimidiatus,
Coris* species and
Hemipteronotus taeniurus, the
sargassum razor fish.

Pomacanthidae - the smaller
angels in the genus *Centropyge*
in a well-established tank with
plenty of algae.

Mullidae - juvenile goat-fishes,
useful scavengers.

Apogonidae - cardinal fishes,
particularly the genus *Apogon,*
but they tend to be noctural. *A.
orbicularis* is a good choice,
active by day.

Gobiidae - small gobies, among
which the neon goby,
Gobiosoma oceanops, the
lemon goby, *Gobiodon citrinus,*
and the fire fish, *Nemateleotris
magnificus,*are to be
recommended.

Bleniidae - many small blennies,
particularly the genera
Ecsenius, Meiacanthus and
Blennius.

Callionymidae - the dragonets,
outstandingly the mandarin fish;
Synchiropus splendidus and the
psychedelic fish, *S. picturatus,*
but they will tend to reduce the
population of small fan worms
and small invertebrates.

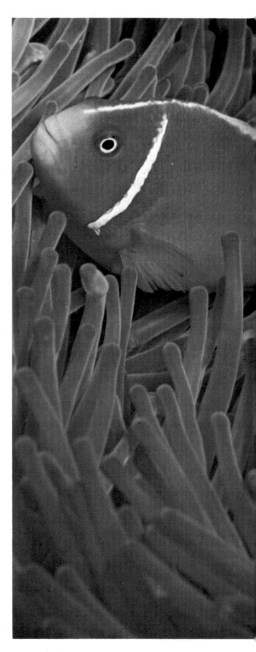

Amphiprion perideraion among the
tentacles of a living, stinging sea
anemone. From the cover of the
second edition of Dr. Gerald R. Allen's
book ANEMONEFISHES. Photo by
Allan Power.

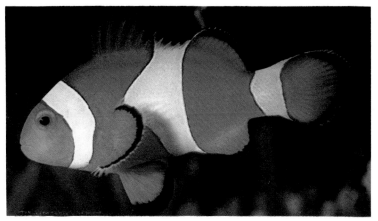

Amphiprion ocellaris.

Dascyllus carneus.

Dascyllus trimaculatus. *These three fishes are suitable for the minireef aquarium.*

Serranidae - only the various *Anthias species* and some hamlets, *Hypolectrus* species; or bigger species on their own or with other large predators.

Grammidae - the basslets, *Gramma* species, but they do tend to hide.

Centriscidae - the shrimp fishes, especially if with a long-spined sea urchin.

Syngnathidae - sea horses and pipefishes, but not with rapid feeders.

Sciaenidae - the high hats, genera *Equetus* and *Eques.*

Monodactylidae - moonfishes, *Monodactylus argenteus* and *M. sebae.*

Theraponidae - the crescent perch, *Therapon jarbua* and its relatives.

Scatophagidae - the tiger scat, *Scatophagus argus* var. *rubifrons* is handsome when small, but grows rapidly.

Pseudochromidae - dottybacks, *Pseudochromis paccagnellae* in particular.

Plesiopidae - the longfins, *Calloplesipos altivelis* and *C. argus* in particular.

With an open-topped aquarium, you must be prepared to lose the occasional fish that will jump out, but with the favorable conditions offered by the miniature reefs and the abundance of hiding places, this is less of a problem than it would be with an ordinary tank.

The fish above is the lovely, peaceful Monodactylus sebae. It is almost equally at home in your minireef, your brackish water aquarium, or in pure freshwater.

Pseudochromis paccagnellae, *named in honor of the famed Italian aquarium designer and manufacturer.*

Pseudochromis perspicillatus.

Pseudochromis flammicauda. *All fishes suitable for the minireef aquarium. These photos from Dr. Burgess's ATLAS OF MARINE AQUARIUM FISHES.*

THE ENCYCLOPEDIA OF MARINE INVERTEBRATES, by a panel of experts.
H-951; ISBN 0-87666-495-8
Hardcover, 5½ X 8, 736 pages; over 600 full-color photos, many line drawings.
This excellent and enormously colorful book ranges widely over the invertebrate field and provides detailed information on the natural history and taxonomy of every invertebrate group of interest to marine aquarists, professional biologists, naturalists, skin-divers and collectors and those involved in the marine aquarium hobby on a commercial level. A superb compilation of vital information and photos, an excellent identification guide.

MARINE INVERTEBRATES AND PLANTS OF THE LIVING REEF, by Dr. Patrick L. Colin.
H-971; ISBN 0-86622-875-6
Hardcover, 5½ X 8½, 512 pages. 430 color photos.
This book is the only complete guide to the inhabitants of a home aquarium miniature reef including marine plants, crabs, starfish, shrimp, corals, anemones, etc. Providing valuable information and photos for the miniature reef aquarist, SCUBA divers, snorkelers and ichthyologists, it shows readers how to identify most reef invertebrates from the Gulf of Mexico, Caribbean Sea, Florida and the tropical Atlantic. This book covers eleven phyla.

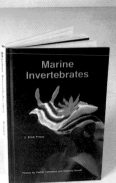

MARINE INVERTEBRATES, by U. Erich Friese.
PS-658 ISBN 0-87666-793-0
Softcover, 8 X 5½, 240 pages;
119 color photos.
This book is intended to give answers to aquarium hobbyists of all levels of experience concerning actual requirements of marine invertebrate animals from an aquarium management point of view plus an overall biological understanding of marine invertebrates. Covers all popular (and many rare) invertebrates, including crabs and lobsters, shrimps, anemones, starfish, molluscs—shown at their bizarrely colorful best. Contains valuable information about which invertebrates are not compatible.

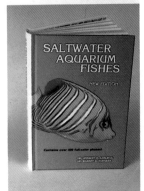

SALTWATER AQUARIUM FISHES, by Dr. Herbert R. Axelrod and Dr. Warren E. Burgess.
H-914; ISBN 0-86622-499-8
Hardcover, 5½ X 8½, 288 pages. Over 400 color photos.
This is a very complete book for the medium-level aquarist who has one or two saltwater tanks and wants to know the best fishes to keep and the best ways to keep them. Modern and up-to-date, the text covers the fishes on a family-by family basis for the convenience of readers. A full chapter is devoted to the coverage of fascinating marine invertebrates.
Comprehensive coverage includes sections on setting up, curing diseases.

DR. BURGESS'S ATLAS OF MARINE AQUARIUM FISHES, by Dr. Warren E. Burgess, Dr. Herbert R. Axelrod and Raymond E. Hunziker III.
H-1100; ISBN 0-86622-896-9
hardcover, 8½ X 11, more than 4600 full-color photos.
This book shows **IN FULL COLOR** not only the popular aquarium fishes but also the oddballs and weirdos. Not only does this book supply photos provided with the most up-to-date scientific names, but the captions indicate the family, range, size and optimum aquarium conditions as well. Also included in this book are family by family write-ups on the aquarium care of marine fishes. Fully indexed by both scientific and common names.

THE MARINE AQUARIUM IN THEORY AND PRACTICE by Dr. Cliff W. Emmens.
PS-735; ISBN 0-86622-054-2
Hardcover, 8½ X 11, 208 pages; 99 black and white photos, 191 color photos.
For the first time, water chemistry, water physics, and theory of a miniature ocean is discussed by Prof. Emmens, chairman of the Veterinary Physiology Department, University of Sydney in Australia. The book takes the reader through the marine aquarium problems step-by-step. Written on a high school level. Includes the Tank and Equipment, Workable Marine Systems, Handling Fishes and Invertebrates, Diseases and Parasites.

EXOTIC MARINE FISHES, by Dr. Herbert R. Axelrod, Dr. Warren E. Burgess, Dr. Cliff W. Emmens.
H-938L (Looseleaf); ISBN 0-87666-103-7
H-938 Hardbound, non-looseleaf) ISBN 0-87666-598-9
Hardcover and looseleaf: 5½ X 8½, 608 pages, 88 black and white photos, 477 full-color photos.
This book is for the avid marine aquarist who has one or more tanks in his home. This is the "bible," brought up-to-date with each edition and maintained as the most current book by the issuance of supplements which illustrate and discuss new fishes. The supplements can be inserted into the looseleaf form or merely used along with the hardbound edition. Complete and authoritative.

MARINE COMMUNITY AQUARIUM: How Fish and Invertebrates Live Together in the Miniature Reef Aquarium, by Dr. Leon P. Zann.
H-1101; ISBN 0-86622-892-6
Hardcover, 5½ X 8½, 416 pages; 342 full-color photos, 83 black and white photos; 33 line drawings.
This book is illustrated with over 340 full-color photos in addition to many monochromes. Dr. Zann has studied how invertebrates and fishes live together in the coral reef and ocean world. Based upon an understanding of this relationship, the marine aquarist is able to correctly plan his miniature reef aquarium. One-of-a-kind photographs make this book interesting and useful.

INDEX